Liesch

TABLE OF CONTENTS

Lisek

Liesch

PROMPT A DAY!

625 Thought-Provoking Writing Prompts Linked to Each Day of the School Year

by Jacqueline Sweeney

SCHOLASTIC
PROFESSIONAL BOOKS

New York • Toronto • London • Auckland • Sydney • Mexico City • New Delhi • Hong Kong

*To Jorie Van Wagenen—school nurse,
"sister," and friend*
—J.S.

Acknowledgments

Many Thanks to: the following teachers for their encouragement and advice—Dotti Griffin, Peggy Hansen, Judy Hutchings, Sally Sroka, Pat Balcom, Daria Murphy, and Rita Sturgis (now a principal!); the librarians who offered me sanctuary as well as access to many valuable resources for my research: in Albany Academy for Girls, Lenape Elementary—New Paltz, NY, and Kathy Stearns of Highland Middle School, NY; ALPS (Alternative Literary Programs) who sponsor many of my writing workshops in school; my editor, Liza Charlesworth; and Marian Reiner, my agent, for her hard work, endurance, and for being "always there" with advice or a sound, quick response.

PHOTO CREDITS: Ducks: © J. B. Aronson; Panda: © United Press International Photo; Flags: © AP/Wide World Photos; Eleanor Roosevelt: © Wide World Photos; United Nations: © Constance Ftera; Mount Rushmore: © Philip Grendreau/Bettmann Archives; Elizabeth Cady Stanton: courtesy of Rhonda Barney Jenkins; George Washington: courtesy of the Trustees of the Boston Public Library; Alvin Ailey: © Wide World Photos; Ben Franklin (p. 66): courtesy of the NYPL Collection; Mahatma Gandhi: © ACME News Pictures; Jackie Robinson: © United Press International Photo; Babe Ruth: courtesy of the National Portrait Gallery/Smithsonian Institution; Winslow Homer: courtesy of the Bowdoin College Museum of Art, Brunswick Maine/Gift of the Homer Family; Alexander Graham Bell: courtesy of ATT; Seals: © Wide World Photos; Hubble Telescope: courtesy of NASA; Harry Truman: U.S. Army Photograph; Thurgood Marshall: © United Press International Photo; Sally Ride: courtesy of NASA; Charles Lindbergh: © United Press International Photo; Ben Franklin (p. 122): © Yale University Art Gallery. POETRY CREDIT: "I'm Brave, I'm Bold" from *New Kid on the Block*. Copyright © by Jack Prelutsky. By permission of Greenwillow Books, a division of William Morrow & Company, Inc.

Cover design by Jaime Lucero and Yuka Iwakoshi
Cover art by Shari Halpern
Edited by Karen Kellaher
Interior design by Liza Charlesworth
Interior illustration by Delana Bettoli
Copyright © 1998 by Jacqueline Sweeney. All rights reserved.

ISBN: 0-590-18738-4
All rights reserved. Printed in the U.S.A.

INTRODUCTION

The "Write Stuff"

"I can't think of anything to write . . . ." If you're like most language arts teachers, that complaint sounds familiar. It's one we've all heard from our students at one time or another, as we encourage them to put pencil to paper. (Or fingertips to keyboard!)

Fortunately, finding fresh and inviting topics to write about does not have to be a headache. This book makes it easy and fun. For *every day* of the school year, I have provided two authentic, meaningful writing prompts: authentic because they are based on actual events in history and contemporary culture, meaningful because they inspire students to make personal connections.

An Invaluable Habit

When I was teaching, I tried to make writing a daily habit for my students. As I quickly learned, that's no easy task in today's classrooms, where changing curricula, state standards, and year-end testing all demand our attention. However, it can be done. With this easy guide, you can introduce writing into even the most crowded curriculum. Rather than take time away from the content areas, the prompts actually tie into what you're teaching.

Throughout the pages of this book, your students will witness the Boston Tea Party and thrill to Babe Ruth's very first home run. They'll celebrate the birthdays of beloved authors and famous Presidents. And they will decide for themselves what makes the best pet and the most useful invention of all time. In responding to such stimulating topics, your students will become better writers and better thinkers.

What You Get with This Book

In writing *Prompt a Day*, I aimed for balance and the occasional change of pace. Some days you will want a serious writing assignment; other days you might enjoy a more humorous prompt. You will find both here. You'll also discover that the prompts cover a wide spectrum of writing styles, from essays to arguments, short stories to shopping lists.

Special Features of This Book

- Daily events (more than one for each day so you can choose what's appropriate for your kids).
- On-level writing prompts that promote higher-order thinking skills.
- Prompts that connect to your science, social studies, music, art, and language arts curricula.
- A multicultural focus, exposing students to celebrations and traditions all over the world.
- An alphabetical index to help you locate a prompt about a specific person.
- Locations for most prompt topics so you can find the calendar events on a map.
- Background information for each prompt that you can read aloud or photocopy for students.

Enjoy! I know that your kids will soon be writing away.

How to Use These Prompts

The prompts are designed for students to respond individually, but can easily be adapted for use in small groups (see "Other Ideas," page 7). Most teachers find that each prompt requires a time commitment of about 10 minutes. I recommend setting aside some time first thing in the morning, when students are fresh and full of ideas.

Before you begin, make sure each student has a notebook or looseleaf binder where he or she can write. Many students like to keep all of their responses in one place so they can watch their writing skills develop over time. In addition, note that a few of the prompts involve research. Scout those out in advance, and be sure to have some resources on hand: Encyclopedias and other reference books, an Internet-ready computer, or relevant trade books are a few examples.

Ready to get started? Here's one approach for using the prompts:

1. Choose one of today's prompts, or read both prompts and allow the students to decide. Write the prompt on the board or distribute photocopies of the prompt to the students. Some prompts may warrant a bit of class discussion before students respond individually.
2. Read aloud the background information provided for today's prompt.
3. Remind students that they can respond in any way they choose; there is no "right" answer.
4. Allow time for students to respond and be available to answer questions.
5. When students are finished, you may choose to collect the responses. This will allow for assessment.

Assessment Tips

1. Collect students' journals periodically and respond to their entries with comments of your own. If you are really strapped for time, I've found that it is possible to rotate the journals: one week I read six to eight journals, the next week I read another six to eight. In this way, you can read every student's journal at least once a month. Know that students hunger for your comments, so try to include substantive, meaningful feedback. Some examples:

> "How did you feel when it was all over, Kate?"

> "What a funny experience, Nilsa!"

> "Robert, I love Mozart too."

2. You can provide a worksheet for children to use once a week to evaluate their own journal work. With your students, decide on the requirements that are important to you. For example, ask students to ask themselves these questions: Did I spell all my words correctly? Did I back up my opinion with examples and evidence?

3. Have students select a few favorite responses to keep in a portfolio. Portfolios are useful for showing a student's progress over time.

Other Ideas

- Feel free to "cheat." You do not have to use the assigned prompts for a given day. Instead, browse through the book until a prompt catches your attention, or use the index to locate a topic that enhances your curriculum for that day.

- Instead of having students respond to prompts individually, break the class into small groups and assign a prompt to each group. Group members must interact to come up with a joint response. Later, have each group present the results of its discussion to the rest of the class.

- Once you have a sense of the kinds of prompts your students like best, you can write some of your own based on local events and people. (A town hero's birthday? The mayoral election campaign? The opening of a new store?) Perhaps your students can offer some original prompts of their own!

AUGUST

August is National Water Quality Month; it is designed to make people more aware of the importance of clean, high-quality water in their daily lives.

Prompt: Brainstorm all the ways your family uses water. Why do you think the water must be clean and free of pollution? Imagine there is a chemical company polluting the water in your neighborhood. Write a letter to the head of the company urging the company to stop polluting.

⊘ AUGUST 15 ⊘

Will Rogers, often called America's "Cowboy Philosopher," died today in 1935. Some of his famous sayings about human nature include:

- "Everybody is ignorant, only on different subjects."
- "Everything is funny, as long as it's happening to somebody else."

Prompt: From the above sayings, choose the one you like best. Explain what you like most about it.

Today is National Relaxation Day, when everyone is encouraged to think of new ways to relax.

Prompt: What do you do when you need to relax? Describe at least two ways that work for you. How do you know when it's time to take it easy? Do you get cranky or have trouble sleeping?

⊘ AUGUST 16 ⊘

Today is Joe Miller's Joke Day, a day to tell a joke in honor of the English comic actor Joseph (Josias) Miller, who was born in 1684, and acted at the famous Drury Theatre in London.

Prompt: What is your favorite joke? Write it down! Who is your favorite funny person? What do you like most about this person's sense of humor?

In Milwaukee, Wisconsin, people celebrate Kite Fly today. On this day, Milwaukee residents gather to fly kites. Some make a kite on the spot; others bring a favorite from home.

Prompt: If you could design a kite in any shape, size, and color, what would it look like? Describe your kite. Does it look like an animal? Is it a geometric design? What does the tail look like? How high will your kite fly?

⊘ AUGUST 17 ⊘

Today in 1807, Robert Fulton and his steamboat, *The Clermont*, made their very first trip: between Albany, New York, and New York City (150 miles). It took 32 hours. The trip was called "Fulton's Folly" (or mistake) by some! But Robert Fulton and his partner, Robert Livingstone, began commercial steamboat service the following year, 1808.

Prompt: Have you ever been made fun of for an idea or creation of your own? (It could be a drawing, the way you dress, etc.) Explain how this made you feel.

David ("Davy") Crockett was born today in 1786 in Hawkins County, Tennessee. He was an American frontiersman, adventurer, soldier, and inspirer of tall tales ("...he kilt him a bear when he was only three," as one song states). Crockett once wrote, "I leave this rule for others when I'm dead. Be always sure you're right, then go ahead."

Prompt: Write your own tall tale. You might begin by filling the blanks in this story starter:

"One day, while hiking in the forest, I saw a _____. It was walking right toward me! I had never seen one with such _____ or that could _____ and _____ before!"

AUGUST 18

Paula Danziger, author of *The Cat Ate My Gymsuit* and *There's a Bat in Bunk Five*, was born today in 1944 in Washington, D.C. Once a month, Paula is the book presenter on a television show in England. One of her presentations was called, "Books You Think Will Make You Puke But Won't." For this show she re-read some old classics she thought she hated (like *Little Women*), and then told kids how great she discovered these books really are.

Prompt: Can you think of a book you thought would make you puke, but didn't? What was it? What made you change your mind about this book?

Today begins Weird Contest Week in Ocean City, New Jersey. There is one contest each day, such as saltwater-taffy sculpting, french-fry sculpting, artistic pie-eating, wet T-shirt throwing, animal impersonations, etc.

Prompt: Create your own category for Weird Contest Week. Be sure to give the rules for your event and the basis on which the judges will determine a winner.

AUGUST 19

By Presidential Proclamation in 1939, today is National Aviation Day, and is celebrated on the birthday of Orville Wright, who piloted the first self-powered flight in history in 1903.

Prompt: Did you ever wish you could fly? Did you ever dream you could? Do you think this wish is what made Orville Wright work so hard to accomplish what he did? How has flying changed our world? Name three ways.

In 1960, the USSR's Sputnik 5 satellite was launched on this date with two special passengers: Belka and Strelka. These passengers became the first living organisms to be recovered from orbit. They were dogs!

Prompt: Why do you think the USSR chose dogs to be the first living things in space? If you were put in charge of selecting the first living things to go into space, which would you choose? Why? What names would you give them?

AUGUST 20

Benjamin Harrison, the 23rd President of the United States, was born today in 1833 in North Bend, Ohio. Benjamin was the grandson of William Henry Harrison, who was the ninth President (1889-1893).

Prompt: Do you think greatness runs in families? Can you think of any other president whose relative was also president? Can you think of any other relatives who achieved great success in the same field of work? (It could be in the fields of music, drama, science, oceanography, etc.)

These long, hot days of late summer are often called "the Dog Days."

Prompt: Why do you think these summer days got that nickname? What would you call these long, lazy days?

AUGUST 21

Hawaii became a state today in 1959, when President Dwight Eisenhower signed a proclamation making it our 50th state. The proclamation had already been approved by a vote of Hawaiian residents.

Prompt: Look up some facts about Hawaii. (If you live there, you can probably come up with these on your own.) Give three good reasons why you think Hawaii would be an interesting place to live.

Each year on this day at Rutgers University, in Brunswick, New Jersey, a special event is held—the Cockroach Derby. There, the fastest roaches in New Jersey race against each other; judges decide which bugs are the best.

Prompt: If you could declare a "Derby Day" in which two animals raced against each other, which animals would you choose? Where would you celebrate the event? Who would be the judge? Be sure to include your rules and requirements for winning.

AUGUST 22

Mexican Fiesta starts today in Milwaukee, Wisconsin. For three days, people celebrate with fun and food. They enjoy the sounds of traditional Mariachi music, a jalapeño-eating contest, and much more.

Prompt: What is your ethnic background? (You might have more than one.) If you were asked to celebrate your cultural background(s) for three days, what events would you plan? You might consider music, special foods, traditional games, etc.

Today is Be an Angel Day, a time to do something nice for someone else.

Prompt: What could you do today (or every day) to make someone else's day easier or happier? Make a list of five ways you could be an "angel."

⦿ AUGUST 23 ⦿

Sir William Wallace (the Scottish patriot played by Mel Gibson in the movie *Braveheart*), died today in London in 1305.

Prompt: What is a patriot? Look it up if you're not sure. Can you think of any other great patriots (from any country) who died for his or her honor and beliefs?

The Great American Duck Race happens today in Deming, New Mexico, where many honors are bestowed, including: World's Richest Duck, Best-Dressed Duck, Duck Queen, Darling Duckling, etc.

Prompt: Imagine you are one of the judges for this Ducky event. Choose two of the categories, and describe the winner of each. Be sure to explain why you chose each one. Have fun!

We're ducky today!

⦿ AUGUST 24 ⦿

Today in A.D. 79, the volcano Mt. Vesuvius erupted, destroying the cities of Pompeii, Stabiae, and Herculaneum. This day is commemorated as Vesuvius Day.

Prompt: What natural disasters (hurricanes, earthquakes, tornadoes, floods, tidal waves, etc.) happen in your area? Have you ever experienced one? Describe your experience. If you have never experienced a disaster, make up a story about the disaster in which you are most interested.

Stepparents' Appreciation Week begins today.

Prompt: Being a stepparent is not an easy job. Unlike Cinderella's stepparent, many try very hard to be kind to their stepchildren. Do you (or does anyone you know) have a stepparent who might be commemorated during this week? Name three good qualities you think every stepmom or stepdad should have.

⦿ AUGUST 25 ⦿

Lane Smith, the illustrator of *The True Story of the Three Little Pigs* and *The Stinky Cheese Man*, was born today in 1959, in Tulsa, Oklahoma. Smith says that he really enjoys creating art for "goofy" stories.

Prompt: Lane Smith says he started out as a quiet kid. Do you know any quiet kids who have a zany sense of humor? Do you ever have days where you feel just plain silly? How do you show your silliness?

Today is Kiss and Make Up Day, a day to fix relationships that need mending.

Prompt: Have you ever been in an argument with a friend or a member of your family? What was the disagreement over? How did you resolve it?

☉ AUGUST 26 ☉

On this day in 1920, the 19th Amendment (the one that gave women the right to vote) became part of the Constitution. In honor of this, Congresswoman Bella Abzug submitted a bill to Congress which became public law in 1974, and celebrates today as Women's Equality Day.

Prompt: Why do you think the United States does not have a day called Men's Equality Day? Explain your answer.

For many students, this time of year is back-to-school time, time to purchase notebooks, pencils, and backpacks, and to meet a new teacher and classmates.

Prompt: What do you like best about school? What do you like least? Describe a first day of school that you remember.

☉ AUGUST 27 ☉

Lyndon Baines Johnson, the 36th President of the U.S. (who led the nation from 1963 to 1969, after John F. Kennedy was assassinated), was born today in 1908 near Stonewall, Texas. In 1964, Johnson said: "The challenge of the next half-century is whether we have the wisdom to use [our] wealth to enrich and elevate our national life, and to advance the equality of American civilization."

Prompt: If you were put in charge of the wealth of the United States for one day, name three ways you would spend it in order to help promote equality in America. (Before answering, think about the many positive ways money can be spent to help people improve their lives.)

The first play ever performed in the North American colonies was presented in Acomac, Virginia, today in 1655. The play was called *Ye Bare and Ye Cubb* and was created by Phillip Alexander Bruce. Three people were arrested for acting in the play. Why? Back then, most colonies had laws forbidding public performances.

Prompt: Can you imagine why the colonies had a law against public performances? Make up your own wacky law that might exist today (a law against lima beans? a law stating that all kids should be able to stay up as late as they want?). Write an essay explaining why you think your law is a good idea.

AUGUST 28

Today in 1963, the 200,000-person Civil Rights March from the South ended in Washington, D.C., where the Reverend Martin Luther King Jr. made his famous "I have a dream…" speech. He said, "I have a dream that my four little children will one day live in a nation where they will not be judged by the color of their skin but by the content of their character."

Prompt: Think about some of your dreams for yourself, your family, and/or your country. After careful thinking, complete two (or more) sentences that begin with the words, "I have a dream that…" If one of your dreams turns into a paragraph or two, that's great!

The illustrator of *Happy Birthday, Martin Luther King*, J. Brian Pinkney, was born today in 1961 in Boston, Massachusetts. Brian says his dad, Jerry Pinkney (the award-winning illustrator of *The Talking Eggs*, etc.), was his idol. "I wanted to be like him," Brian says. Brian also says his father never competes with him. He just offers advice and encouragement. "That's probably because he is such a nice guy," Brian says.

Prompt: Is there anyone in your life whom you would consider an idol? (It could be a parent; it could also be someone you don't personally know, like a famous musician or sports star.) Which of this person's qualities inspires you the most?

AUGUST 29

In just a few short weeks, summer will be drawing to a close.

Prompt: Think about your summer. Describe your best experience. Was it a special vacation? A day with friends?

Hog Capital of the World Festival begins today in Kewanee, Illinois, where events include the World's Largest Pork Chop barbecue and a four-mile run (Hog Stampede).

Prompt: If you were asked to design a fair or festival celebrating an animal or product from your state (a horse, pine tree, special flower, insect, etc.), what "beast" or product would you honor? Describe three of your festival's events. Be sure to include the food you'd feature!

AUGUST 30

In Woodstock, Vermont, people are celebrating Children's Day. Since Vermont has many farming areas, Children's Day is celebrated with traditional activities: corn shelling, 19th-century games such as firewood sawing, ice cream and butter making, even an old-fashioned spelling bee!

Prompt: If you could design your own Children's Day, what events would you choose to celebrate? Name at least three. Give the reasons for your choices.

The Keep the Flame Alive Storytelling Contest happens today in Millersport, Ohio.

Prompt: Have you ever heard a story told by a storyteller? If so, describe your experience. How would you compare *hearing* a story to reading one? (If you have never seen or heard a storyteller perform, think about the times your parents or teachers read aloud to you.)

AUGUST 31

William Saroyan, a Pulitzer Prize-winning American author, was born today in Chicago, Illinois, in 1907. A month before he died (in 1981), Saroyan gave reporters a final statement—to be published only after his death. It said: "Everybody has got to die, but I have always believed an exception would be made in my case. Now what?"

Prompt: If you could give reporters a statement to be published only after your death, what would it say? Remember, people might remember you more for this statement than for anything you've accomplished in your life!

On this day in 1997, Princess Diana of Wales was killed in an automobile accident. Diana left behind two sons.

Prompt: Has anyone close to you ever passed away? (It could be someone famous, like Princess Diana or Elvis Presley). Write the three best things you remember about this person. What three things would *you* like to be remembered for?

SEPTEMBER

September is SAVE THE TIGER MONTH, and is devoted to preserving the endangered Siberian and Bengal tiger species.

Prompt: If you had the power to name one month as "Save the_____ Month," which species of animal would you choose? What activities would you design to promote public awareness of your campaign to preserve this creature? For example, you might organize a nationwide art contest for kids, or have fund-raisers.

⊘ SEPTEMBER 1 ⊘

French explorer Jacques Cartier died on this day in 1557. In his search for the Northwest Passage (a quick route to the Orient), Cartier instead discovered the St. Lawrence River and explored Canada's coastal areas. He eventually took possession of this country in the name of France.

Prompt: Who is your favorite explorer? Write an essay explaining what this person accomplished and why you think he or she is so great. Remember, some explorers, like Cartier, lived hundreds of years ago, but others are alive today (for example, some of the first American astronauts).

___

On the first Monday in September, we celebrate Labor Day, a time to remember and recognize all workers in the U.S. and Canada. The holiday started with a parade in New York City in 1882 to argue for the rights of workers.

Prompt: Choose one worker in your community and explain why the community needs his or her work. If you'd like, write a letter to that person in honor of Labor Day to thank him or her for all that hard work!

⊘ SEPTEMBER 2 ⊘

Today in 1948, Christa McAuliffe was born. This 37-year-old high school teacher from Concord, New Hampshire, would have been the first "ordinary citizen" in space, but she died along with six crew members when the space shuttle *Challenger* exploded on January 28, 1986.

Prompt: Can you think of any other people who have risked their lives in order to explore new territories, on Earth or elsewhere? Do you think their risk-taking was worth it?

___

The Great Fire of London happened in England today in 1666. It began in the house of a baker and burned out of control for three days and nights. It eventually destroyed two thirds of the city. The 436 acres included 13,200 homes, 89 churches, 430 streets, and the city gates.

Prompt: Luckily, it would be rather difficult for a fire like this one to happen today in any U.S. city or town. That's because homes today are often better constructed to withstand fire, we have well-trained and well-equipped fire departments, and most people know their fire safety rules. For example, we can call 911 or the fire department in case of fire. How many other ways can you think of to prevent fires, and to keep people safe if a fire does start?

● **SEPTEMBER 3** ●

Aliki Brandenberg was born today in 1929 in Wildwood Crest, New Jersey, and grew up to become the author/illustrator of many books, including *How a Book Is Made* and *Manners*. Her fame was predicted by her kindergarten teacher, who recognized her artistic abilities and told her parents she'd be an artist someday.

Prompt: Is there anyone in your life who has encouraged you to pursue one of your talents? (It could be music, sports, art, cooking, etc.) Explain how this encouragement makes you feel. Is there anyone in your life (a brother or sister or cousin or friend) whose talent you might encourage? Explain.

The Treaty of Paris was signed today in France in 1783, ending the Revolutionary War between Britain and the United States. The American signers were John Adams, Benjamin Franklin, and John Jay.

Prompt: Imagine you are one of the signers of this Treaty to end the War for Independence. You have been fighting for your country's freedom for many long, hard years. And now that freedom is yours. Think of how tired and proud you must be feeling about now, then pretend you are writing in your diary the night of September 3, 1783. What would you say?

● **SEPTEMBER 4** ●

Author Joan Aiken was born today in 1924 in Sussex, England. This author of *The Teeth of the Gale* and *The Wolves of Willoughby Chase*, explains that since she was a girl of five, she has carried a small notebook with her everywhere she goes. Besides keeping a notebook, Joan has this advice for every writer: "Try to write a few pages every day. Never write anything that bores you. Collect interesting stories from the newspapers. Think of the end of a story before you start it. Read as much as you possibly can..."

Prompt: Which piece of Joan Aiken's advice do you find most helpful? Why do you think she says, "Never write anything that bores you"?

Today is Newspaper Carrier Day in honor of Barney Flaherty, age 10, of New York City, who became the first "newsboy" in America.

Prompt: Do you know any newspaper carriers? Do you think you would like this job? What other kinds of jobs can kids do to earn money?

⊘ SEPTEMBER 5 ⊘

On this day in 1774, the First Continental Congress opened in Philadelphia, Pennsylvania.

Prompt: Imagine that you are in charge of the first meeting of the Continental Congress (with American colonists discussing how they feel about being ruled by the British and what the future may bring). Think about how the colonists are being taxed (paying money to England) without ever having a say about any of the laws the British government is imposing on them. What do you think your first point of discussion would be? Do you think you'd be more likely to be quiet and listen, or stand up and shout? Explain your answer.

Today is celebrated as Be Late For Something Day, designed to release the tensions of people who are constantly stressed over the need to be on time.

Prompt: Are you the kind of person who needs a day like this? What, if any,

events in your life would it be alright to be late for? What events would it definitely not be alright to be late for?

⊘ SEPTEMBER 6 ⊘

The *Mayflower* sailed for America today in 1620. The Pilgrims on board the ship included 74 men and 28 women in search of religious freedom.

Prompt: Imagine dropping everything and leaving for a new land thousands of miles away. Name two things the Pilgrims were thinking about during their journey? What kinds of things do you think they brought with them? What five things would you bring if you were moving to a new land and could not bring everything you own?

By a 1986 Presidential Proclamation, this is Federal Lands Cleanup Day.

Prompt: If you were in charge of "Local School Cleanup Day," what's the first order you would give? (You might want to take a minute to look around your school, inside and out, before deciding.) What do you think the second and third orders of the day might be?

⊘ SEPTEMBER 7 ⊘

The famous American painter Grandma Moses, or Anna Mary Robertson Moses, was born today in Greenwich, New York, in 1860.

Prompt: Grandma Moses didn't even start painting until the age of 78, and she is famous today. What advice do you think she would give someone who is afraid to try something new?

National Grandparents' Day is celebrated this week (by a 1979 Presidential Proclamation declared it the first Sunday after Labor Day).

Prompt: If your favorite grandparent or other older person was standing in front of you now, what might you say to thank him or her? Think about this person's qualities and what he or she means to you.

✪ SEPTEMBER 8 ✪

Jack Prelutsky, author of *New Kid On the Block* and *Something Big Has Been Here*, was born today in 1940 in Brooklyn, New York. Jack admits that as a boy he thought poetry was like liver. He "couldn't stand the stuff." Today he is one of the most popular children's poets in America! Here's one of his poems from the book *New Kid on the Block*.

I'm Bold, I'm Brave

I'm bold, I'm brave, I know no fear.
I'm gallant as a buccaneer.
Is that a hornet by my ear?
Gangway! I'm getting out of here!

Prompt: Do you think this poem is funny? If so, why? Now write your own funny poem about someone you know very well—yourself!

Today is United Nations International Literacy Day.

Prompt: Can you imagine growing up and not knowing how to read? How do you think you'd feel if you weren't able to read a book, or the directions to a new game, or road signs? What if you were an adult and still couldn't read? This happens. Name three things you might do to promote literacy (learning to read) in your family, town, or school. For example, you might suggest some great books for the library.

✪ SEPTEMBER 9 ✪

Today is California Admission Day, the day in 1850 when California was admitted to the Union and became the 31st state.

Prompt: Find out when your state was admitted to the Union. Pretend you are living back then and plan a party to celebrate this event. Think about the kinds of things that make your state famous and include them in your celebration. For example, Georgia is famous for its peaches, so you might celebrate its admission day with everything imaginable that can be made with peaches.

The first giant panda to be born in captivity (a zoo) was born today in China in 1963.

Prompt: What do you like most about zoos? Is there anything you don't like about zoos? When you go to the zoo, which animal do you want to see first? Explain what you like most about this animal. If you have never been to a zoo, tell about the animal you'd most like to see up close.

September 10

The sewing machine was patented today in 1846.

Prompt: Do you think the sewing machine was an important invention? Why or why not? What would we do without the sewing machine? What are some other inventions that you think are important? Why?

Swap Ideas Day is today, and has been set aside to encourage people to use their creative imaginations to help themselves and others.

Prompt: Ask a friend or classmate to share one problem or challenge he or she faces today or this week. Does he think the social studies homework is difficult? Is she running for class president? Now write down three suggestions that might help your friend face the challenge. Finally, share your ideas with the other person.

September 11

Benjamin Franklin wrote one of his most often quoted lines today in 1773: "There was never a good war or a bad peace."

Prompt: What is your opinion of this quote? Do you agree? Disagree? Why?

Singer Jenny Lind, also known as the "Swedish Nightingale," appeared in concert in New York City today in 1850. Seven thousand people came to hear her, and the first ticket sold cost $225.

Prompt: That $225 ticket is equivalent to several thousand dollars today. Can you think of any group or performer you would be willing to pay that much money to see? (If you had that much money, of course!) Why do you think people are willing to pay such high prices to see celebrities in person?

September 12

Today in 1954, the TV program *Lassie* first aired. It was about a dog who lived with a family on a farm. Lassie was brave and intelligent; she sometimes even saved people's lives.

Prompt: Imagine you are starring in a T.V. program that features an animal as your best friend. Which animal would you choose for the role? What would you name it?

Runner Jesse Owens, the star of the 1936 Olympics at Berlin (he won four track-and-field medals, including the 100-meter run and the long jump), was born today in 1913 in Oakville, Alabama.

Prompt: What athlete from the past or present inspires you to be your best? Why? If you could compete in the Olympics, which sport would you choose?

September 13

Clara Schumann, a German composer and pianist who greatly influenced the music of Robert Schumann (her husband), as well as Johannes Brahms, was born today in 1819. Clara was known as "Queen of the Piano" for her incredible playing abilities. Her concerts were so popular, the police had to be called in for crowd control!

Prompt: Do you play an instrument? Which one? If you could be called "King" or "Queen" of any instrument, which one would you choose? Why?

The idea for the "Star Spangled Banner" was planted on this night in 1814. Francis Scott Key was aboard a ship in Baltimore Harbor during the British attack on Fort Henry. Anxiously watching the battle all night, he was inspired at seeing the American flag still flying over the fort the next morning. That's when he wrote the verses of our national anthem.

Prompt: Do you know all the words to our national anthem? Do you find it difficult to sing? Would you want to change it? Why or why not?

⌀ SEPTEMBER 14 ⌀

Author/illustrator John Steptoe was born today in 1950 in Brooklyn, New York. This author of *Stevie* and *Mufaro's Beautiful Daughters* explores family and city life in nearly all of his books, and is one of the first children's book authors to focus on black life in the city. He grew up in the Bedford-Stuyvesant section of Brooklyn and writes of things he knew and dreamed of, things he wants to say to children.

Prompt: If you were asked to write about something *you* know about and would like to say to others (adults or children), what would you choose to write about? (It might be a growing-up experience with stepbrothers or stepsisters [as in *Stevie*], or it could be about something you like to do more than anything else, or about something you believe in.)

National Pet Memorial Day is today; it's a day to remember a person's deceased pet and the importance of that pet to its owner's family.

Prompt: Do you have fond feelings for a pet that died (yours or someone else's)? Remember, this pet can be from any species that you love: a lizard, a fish, a frog, etc. Share a story about this pet.

⌀ SEPTEMBER 15 ⌀

Jumbo, the famous elephant, died on this date in 1885.

Prompt: If you were asked to prepare a funeral for an elephant, how would you do it? Be sure to include at least four steps (or details) ranging from burial arrangements to an appropriate funeral song. Have you or has anyone you know ever had a funeral for a beloved pet? Describe how you or your friend said good-bye.

Greenpeace was founded today in 1971. This environmental organization is committed to making the world a "greener" and more peaceful place. It was founded by two people from the "Don't Make a Wave" committee of Vancouver, British Columbia, Canada, who believed that even a small group of determined people can change the behavior of "even the overwhelmingly powerful" by being on the scene, watching, and drawing attention to any environmental abuse whatever the risk.

Prompt: Do you agree or disagree with the Greenpeace philosophy? Can you think of a cause that would inspire you to act according to its beliefs?

✪ SEPTEMBER 16 ✪

Author Joanne Ryder was born today in 1946 in Lake Hiawatha, New Jersey. Joanne loves observing nature and all its creatures. Where else would *The Snail's Spell* and *Sea Elf* come from? She once said: "Going for a walk instantly calms me down. It gives me a peaceful feeling."

Prompt: What calms you down? Describe two things you like to do to get that "peaceful feeling."

Chusok, or the Autumn Harvest Thanksgiving Moon Festival, is a gala celebration by Koreans everywhere (observed on the 8th full moon of the lunar calendar). At this time, Koreans express thanks to guardian spirits for another year of rich crops, and also pay their respects to their ancestors by visiting their tombs and leaving food. "Moon cake" is a traditional food for this day made of rice, chestnuts, and jujube fruits.

Prompt: Do you know who any of your ancestors are? If you could pay your respects to your ancestors, what food would you leave for them? Why did you choose this particular food?

✪ SEPTEMBER 17 ✪

By a 1953 Presidential Proclamation, today became Citizenship Day, which appropriately coincides with Constitution Week.

Prompt: A constitution is a legal document that contains a system of rules to protect its citizens. The rules are called laws, and citizens follow the laws in order for a country to run. If you suddenly found yourself in charge of a brand new country, with the job of making the constitution for its citizens, what would your first three laws be? Explain why you chose them.

Clownfest begins today in Seaside Heights, New Jersey, where clowns from all over the country come together for five days of performances and competitions.

Prompt: There are many kinds of clowns: sad ones, pretty ones, mischievous and silly ones, all with differing costumes and make-up. If you were asked to design yourself as a clown, which kind would you be? Describe your costume and the way your make-up looks: Is your face white or blue? Do you have a big red nose? Furry eyebrows? Do you carry a horn? A chicken? Have fun!

SEPTEMBER 18

On this day in 1830, the first locomotive, the *Tom Thumb*, lost a nine-mile race with a horse—between Riley's Tavern just outside Baltimore, Maryland, and a spot inside the city. In fact, a boiler leak kept the train from ever finishing the race. So the "Iron Horse" (an early nickname for trains) was outpaced by a horse!

Prompt: Think for a moment about life in America in the 1700s. Name at least two ways early Americans might have depended on their horses. Now think about life today. How many different kinds of transportation do we use in our daily lives? What are the advantages and disadvantages of each one? Which is your favorite? Why?

Today is National Student Day, a great time to honor students like yourself, from preschool through university.

Prompt: Do you think your community should treat students in a special way on this day? For example, should the local candy store provide discounts? Should schools give extra recess time on this day? Outline your ideas for celebrating Student Day.

(Name at least four ways you'd like to celebrate.)

SEPTEMBER 19

Today in 1783, the Montgolfier brothers sent up the first balloon with live creatures on board: a sheep, a rooster, and a duck.

Prompt: Why do you think the Montgolfier brothers sent up animals before they tried to go up in the balloon themselves? Do you think it was fair? Why or why not?

Mickey Mouse was introduced for the first time today in a 1928 cartoon called *Steamboat Willie* (in black and white, of course!) at the Colony Theater in New York.

Prompt: What is it about Mickey Mouse that has kept him popular for all these years? List your favorite Mickey qualities. If you don't like Mickey, choose a different cartoon character and list his or her good qualities.

SEPTEMBER 20

The Equal Rights For Women Party was formed on this day in 1884, to ensure equal representation in Presidential elections. Their candidate for President was Mrs. Belva Lockwood. The Vice-Presidential candidate was Marietta Stow.

Prompt: Why do you think women had to form their own party in order to nominate a female Presidential candidate? Do you think there will ever be a woman President of the U.S.? Why or why not?

Today is National Kids Day; designed to increase people's awareness of the importance and dignity of children everywhere.

Prompt: If you were designing a poster to advertise National Kids Day, and were told to include: 1) three great children's qualities you think people should be aware of, and 2) three actions people might take to make children feel more valued, which qualities and actions would you include?

◎ SEPTEMBER 21 ◎

Chief Joseph, the Nez Perce chief, died on this day in 1904. Born in 1840 in Wallowa Valley, Oregon Territory, Chief Joseph led his people on a 1,000-mile journey to Canada in an attempt to escape war and unfair resettlement on a reservation. After three months of difficult travel, his people were surrounded by soldiers only 40 miles from Canada (and freedom) and were sent to a reservation.

Prompt: Imagine you had traveled for many days (more than 900 miles), and were captured just 40 miles short of your goal and freedom. How would you feel? What would you say to your captors?

Today begins National Dog Week, to focus attention on the importance of dogs to people, as well as stress the need for proper care and humane treatment of these loyal animals.

Prompt: Describe your favorite dog. (It might belong to someone else, or be a famous dog from a book or movie.) What qualities make this dog important

to you? If you were a dog, what three things would you most like your owner to remember to do?

◎ SEPTEMBER 22 ◎

In the late 1800s, the inventor of the ice cream cone, Italo Marchiony, emigrated from Italy to the United States. On this day in 1903, his application for a patent for an ice cream pastry mold was officially filed. (His first cone was made of paper!)

Prompt: How do you think Marchiony thought of the ice cream cone? (Hint: Remember the famous phrase, "Necessity is the mother of invention.") Name five foods you are glad were invented (be sure to include toppings and sauces!) Which is your favorite?

Today is Dear Diary Day, which encourages *everyone* (not just professional writers!) to put their thoughts and feelings down on paper.

Prompt: Have you ever kept a journal or diary? Name three reasons why writing down your thoughts and feelings is a *good* thing to do.

⊘ SEPTEMBER 23 ⊘

This is the first day of National Imperfection Week, which is a celebration of people's right to be imperfect.

Prompt: We have imperfections because we are human. Think about some of your imperfections. Do you procrastinate (put off doing things that need to be done)? Do you eat too much junk food? Are you jealous of your little brother or sister? Then answer the following:

1. List two of your imperfections. (Now forgive yourself for simply being human like everybody else.)

2. What might you do to overcome your imperfections?

The planet Neptune was discovered today in 1846. It is the eighth planet from the sun (about 30 times as far from the sun as the Earth is) and takes 164.8 years to revolve around the sun.

Prompt: What is your favorite planet? Explain why you like this planet the best. (For its temperature? Colors? Rings?)

⊘ SEPTEMBER 24 ⊘

Jim Henson, creator of many of the puppets on the Muppet Show and Sesame Street, was born today in 1936 in Greenville, Mississippi.

Prompt: You probably know of Henson's work: Kermit the Frog, Miss Piggy, Big Bird, Bert and Ernie, Oscar the Grouch, etc. Which character is your favorite? If you could be one of these puppets, which one would you choose? Give the reasons for your choice.

Today is National Win With Courtesy Day. Courtesy is politeness.

Prompt: Can you remember the last polite thing you said or did? Who would you most want to loan a pencil to:

1. The person who says, "Give me a pencil NOW!"

2. The person who says, "May I borrow a pencil, please?"

Explain how #1 makes you feel.

⊘ SEPTEMBER 25 ⊘

The first American newspaper was published today in 1690 in Boston, Massachusetts, by Benjamin Harrison. It was called *Publick Occurrences Both Foreign and Domestick*. Unfortunately, it was the first and only edition. The British, who ruled America at the time, considered this first newspaper offensive and ordered it stopped.

Prompt: Do you ever read a newspaper? What kind of information do you get from it? If you started a newspaper, what would you call it? What would be the subject of your first story?

Today in 1789, the first session of America's First Congress met in New York and voted ten amendments, or additions, to the Constitution. These additions are now known as the Bill of Rights.

Prompt: Think about the rights you enjoy as an American citizen. Name your three favorites. Why do you think the Congress wanted to add such rights to the Constitution?

SEPTEMBER 26

Johnny Appleseed was born today in 1774 in Leominster, Massachusetts. Otherwise known as John Chapman, he was regarded as a great medicine man by Native Americans for his knowledge of herbs and his willingness to share his knowledge to heal others. A friend of wild animals, John Chapman is best known for roaming the countryside planting apple seeds from which many of New England's apple orchards are said to have begun.

Prompt: If you could choose the seeds from one fruit or vegetable to carry and plant as far as you could walk in a year, what would you choose to plant? Give the reason for your choice.

For many parts of the U.S., this time of the year is harvest time, when wheat and other crops are gathered from the fields. Once the work is done, there are festivals and other celebrations.

Prompt: Imagine you are a newspaper reporter about to interview a local farmer at harvest time. What five questions would you ask? How do you predict the farmer would answer?

SEPTEMBER 27

Author/illustrator Bernard Waber was born today in 1924 in Philadelphia, Pennsylvania. This author of *Lyle, Lyle Crocodile* and *Ira Sleeps Over* says that as he was growing up, he learned a lot from his brothers and sister. One brother loved reading and chess, one brother liked to draw and write, while his sister played the piano and wrote love letters for others. All these things inspired him.

Prompt: Name something you've learned from a brother or sister (for example, it could be a song, how to draw, or how to tie your shoes). If you don't have a brother or sister, how about a cousin or friend? Can you think of any knowledge or experiences of your own that you've shared with a brother/sister or cousin/friend?

Today is Pancake Day in Centerville, Iowa.

Prompt: There are a zillion possibilities for pancakes (buckwheat, blueberry, chocolate with cherries, shrimp and pickle, etc.). How many kinds of pancakes can you think of? (Don't be afraid to use your imagination!) Make a list!

SEPTEMBER 28

Jonas Salk, the American scientist who developed a vaccine against polio, was born today in 1914.

Prompt: Before Salk developed his vaccine, many people died or were crippled by polio. It was a disease with no cure (even President Franklin Roosevelt was stricken). No one knew what caused it and everyone feared it. Can you think of any other diseases in the world today for which we have no cure? Can you imagine how people will feel when we get a cure?

Today is National Good Neighbor Day, to encourage understanding and kindness toward our fellow people: beginning with the neighbor next door!

Prompt: Name three kind acts you might do today to help your neighbors. (It could be simply sharing a pencil with the person next to you.)

● SEPTEMBER 29 ●

Today is the feast of St. Michael (prince of guardian angels) in the Greek and Roman Catholic Churches. This feast celebrates the same angel that John Travolta played in the movie *Michael*. The feast is celebrated all over Central Pennsylvania as a tribute to the ancient feast and old English proverb, "If you eat goose on Michaelmas Day, you will not want for money all year."

Prompt: Pretend a feast is to be celebrated on your birthday—named after you, of course, such as "Beth Day," "Jose Day," or "Kristin Day." Choose the food you'd like to be served to commemorate you: spinach? liver? hamburgers? Create a feast day for yourself. Start out by saying, On (day in calendar), we will celebrate (your name) Day. Everyone will eat (food) and wear (whatever you want). Be sure to include games and activities worthy of your day!

The Fall Foliage Festival begins today in parts of Vermont. These areas welcome many visitors to come see Vermont's famous fall leaves. The leaves change because they are finished making food for the tree, so they no longer need the green chlorophyll. The pretty colors are hidden underneath the green!

Prompt: Have you ever seen colorful fall leaves? Write a folk tale to explain why leaves change color. (A folk tale is a story that people make up, often to explain something in nature.) Use your imagination. It can be funny, mysterious, or even sad. Think first—then have fun!

● SEPTEMBER 30 ●

On this day in 1927, baseball great Babe Ruth set a home run record: He hit his 60th home run for the season. Although his record has since been broken, Babe Ruth remains a baseball legend.

Prompt: Have you ever had a shining moment, like Babe Ruth's home run? Think about your experiences in school, sports, etc. Write a story about your moment. (Remember, it could be a small moment, like learning long division or getting an "A" in spelling.)

On this day in 1846, the first tooth was extracted with the use of anesthesia (ether), by Dr. William Morton of Charleston, Massachusetts.

Prompt: Is anyone you know afraid of the dentist? Dream up an invention that would make dentist visits either more pleasant or unnecessary. Is it a toothpaste that super-cleans teeth? A movie screen attached to the dentist's chair? Have fun!

OCTOBER

October is one month that many organizations have chosen as *their* month. Some examples are:

- Computer Learning Month
- Adopt-a-Shelter Dog
- Consumer Information Month
- Do-It-Yourself Month
- Family History Month
- National Car Care Month
- National Clock Month
- National Communicate With Your Kid Month

- National Dental Hygiene Month
- National Dessert Month
- National Disability Employment Awareness Month
- National Pizza Month
- National Roller Skating Month
- Vegetarian Awareness Month
- National Crime Prevention Month

Prompt: Think about the above list and then choose the two that you consider most important for national consideration during the month of October. Give your reasons for each choice, then create one activity (this might include an advertising campaign, slogan, or song, etc.) you think would best celebrate each one.

OCTOBER 1

Jimmy Carter (he legally changed his name from James Earl), the 39th President of the U.S., was born today in 1924 in Plains, Georgia. A man committed to women's rights and the rights of the poor, Jimmy Carter has spent his retirement years actively pitching in on construction sites to upgrade housing for those who can't afford their own homes. A skilled negotiator, President Carter still volunteers his time to travel to troubled spots throughout the world where he might assist countries in making or keeping peace.

Prompt: What qualities do you think a person must have to help countries—or everyday people—make peace? Do you have suggestions for solving conflicts without yelling or fighting?

Rosh Hashana (the Jewish New Year) begins at sundown around this time of the year. It marks the beginning of ten days of praying for forgiveness of wrongdoings.

Prompt: Can you think of a time when someone forgave you for doing something wrong? How did it feel?

OCTOBER 2

The first week in October is Universal Children's Week, a time when people all over the globe talk about the needs of children.

Prompt: Name the top ten things you believe all children need, regardless of where they live.

Today is National Custodial Worker Day, celebrated in honor of the men and women who clean up after us in schools and office buildings everywhere.

Prompt: We often take custodial workers for granted and needlessly add to their workload each day. Name at least three ways you can make your school custodian's job easier. (Consider classrooms, the cafeteria, rest rooms, hallways, etc.)

○ OCTOBER 3 ○

Today begins Pickled Pepper Week. It's a holiday created by the companies that sell hot and sweet peppers!

Prompt: Pickled peppers are the topic of a famous tongue twister. Maybe you know it: "Peter Piper picked a peck of pickled peppers." Try to say this twister aloud. What do you think makes those simple words so hard to say? Write a tongue twister of your own, about peppers or any topic you like.

Today in 1952, the show *Wheel of Fortune* first aired on TV. If you've ever seen the show, you know the contestants must guess names, words, phrases, and titles by guessing letters in the words. Guessing the right letters can mean thousands of dollars!

Prompt: What is your favorite game show? What do you like most about this show? (If you don't have a favorite show, what is your favorite game?)

○ OCTOBER 4 ○

Rutherford B. Hayes, the 19th President of the U.S., was born today in 1877 in Delaware, Ohio. Hayes was a lawyer and a soldier who won the Presidency by only one electoral vote. Why? He hated campaigning, or trying to persuade people to vote for him. When he left office he was respected for his honesty. But others hated him because he was so fair. (For example, he would not give government jobs to his friends; instead he would hire whomever was best for the job.)

Prompt: Do you think it would be possible to be president of *anything* today (a class, a company, club, the U.S.) and not be expected to give favors to people— especially friends who helped you get elected? If you were President, do you think you might be tempted to give a friend or relative a government job? Is that fair?

In early October, people celebrate Get Organized Week. It's a good time to clean up your bedroom and your desk at school.

Prompt: Do you consider yourself an organized person? Describe one thing you do to organize your belongings. If you are usually disorganized, describe one thing you could do to be better organized.

◢ OCTOBER 5 ◣

Fire Prevention Week is always the first or second week in October.

Prompt: Name two precautions you might take in your home to make it safe from fire. What do you think is the best advice you could give a younger brother or sister to keep him or her safe from fire?

The United States Supreme Court returns to work at this time of year, after a summer break. The Court reviews important legal cases from all over the country. The decisions of the nine justices, or judges, often affect the entire nation.

Prompt: Do you think you would like to be a judge? What qualities do you suppose a judge must have?

◢ OCTOBER 6 ◣

Thor Heyerdahl was born today in 1914 in Larvik, Norway. In April, 1947, he sailed from South America on a raftlike boat called the *Kon Tiki* that was built out of balsa wood. Thor wanted to prove that the inhabitants of a Pacific Island called Fatu Hiva could have come from as far away as South America. Everyone said he was crazy. So he and a crew of five proved everyone wrong, since they made the trip just as their ancestors could have—in 101 days.

Prompt: Have you ever been laughed at for one of your ideas? Did the laughing make you change your mind about your idea? Why or why not?

◢ OCTOBER 7 ◣

This marks the beginning of National Newspaper Week.

Prompt: Do you read a newspaper? Which sections do you read first? Why?

This is a popular time for apple picking in many parts of the country.

Prompt: Have you ever visited an apple orchard? Describe your experience. How many things can you think of that are made with apples? Make a list.

OCTOBER 8

Barthe DeClements, author of *Sixth Grade Can Really Kill You* and *No Place For Me*, was born on this day in 1920 in Seattle, Washington. Barthe says that she was first a teacher, and then a guidance counselor, and began writing books because she thought they might help children solve problems.

Prompt: Can you think of any books you've read that might help someone solve a problem? Which book was it? How do you think it helped?

Today is National Children's Day, a day to ensure that all children receive the protection, care, and guidance that they need *every* day in order to become honest, hardworking citizens when they grow up.

Prompt: Think carefully, then list the three most important ways you think a parent might celebrate National Children's Day. Now list the three ways you think a teacher might best celebrate National Children's Day. Be sure to include things you think people should do for their children all year long.

OCTOBER 9

Today is Leif Erikson Day, in honor of the Norse explorer who sailed west from Greenland around A.D. 1000 to find the strange land he had been hearing about. This land turned out to be North America, which Leif named "Vinland." Of course, neither Spain nor Christopher Columbus knew about Leif's discovery, or they wouldn't have been able to claim "America" for Spain nearly 500 years later.

Prompt: Why do you think no one heard about Leif Erikson's voyage to America for so many years? (Think about how different the lives of human beings must have been in the year 1000). If an explorer found a new land today, how might the news get out?

Today begins The National Shrimp Festival in Gulf Shores, Alabama, to salute the shrimping industry.

Prompt: Many human qualities are described in terms of animals; for example "she has eyes like an *eagle*," or "he's in a *crabby* mood" today. How do you think the term "shrimp" came to be? How do you think it makes others feel to be called "shrimp"?

OCTOBER 10

On this day in 1813, Guiseppe Verdi, the famous Italian composer of the operas *Aida*, *Rigoletto*, and *la Traviata*, was born. Verdi was not just a great composer and musician, he was also a farmer. He began a special tradition that combined his love for music with his love for the land: Every time he completed an opera, Verdi planted a tree.

Prompt: What do you think of Verdi's tradition? Do you have a special tradition? If you could make up a tradition for yourself, what would it be? (Remember, a tradition doesn't have to be big. It can be as simple as planting a flower for every new person born in your family, or marking the doorframe for every inch you grow, etc.)

Yom Kippur, or Day of Atonement, is a sacred Jewish holy day falling on the 10th day of the seventh month (on the Hebrew calendar). This is a day of prayer for the forgiveness of sins committed during the year. In European countries, Yom Kippur is often celebrated by going to the homes of friends, neighbors, relatives (and enemies!) to announce any wrongdoings and beg forgiveness for all sins of the past year. Next, people wish one another to be written and sealed into the *Book of the Living*, where the names of all good people are kept.

Prompt: If you could visit anyone in the world today to ask forgiveness for a wrong you feel you have committed against him or her during the past year (it could be for *anything*—even forgetting to return a borrowed pencil, etc.), whom would you visit? What would you say?

⊘ OCTOBER 11 ⊘

E leanor Roosevelt was born today in New York City in 1884. She was the niece of President Theodore Roosevelt and the wife of Franklin D. Roosevelt (our 32nd President). Eleanor actively campaigned for her husband and spoke out for the rights of women (and anyone poor or suffering). She did not act like a traditional woman in the early 1900s in America. She was the first wife of a President to ever give her own White House news conference and became known with great affection as "First Lady of the World."

Prompt: If you could be known in future years as "first lady" or "first man" of the world, what would you like to be known for? (You may list more than one thing!) Be sure to explain why you chose what you did.

M any animals migrate at this time of year. Geese fly south to warm areas like Florida. Mountain animals descend, or drop down, to lower, warmer altitudes.

Prompt: If you were an animal, would you migrate each year? If so, where would you choose to go? Why?

⊘ OCTOBER 12 ⊘

C olumbus Day is celebrated today in America and most Spanish-speaking countries to honor the arrival of Columbus on October 12, 1492, at Guanahani, one of the Bahama Islands. Columbus renamed the island "El Salvador" and claimed it for Spain. A little-known fact about that arrival is that it actually happened on October 13. But because susperstition said the number 13 was unlucky, Columbus was persuaded to change the date in his log! He worried that the number 13 would scare away people who might help pay for future voyages.

Prompt: Pretend you want to take an expedition to an unknown land, and need to convince people to give you millions of dollars to finance your trip. You have to explain to your investors why this trip will be worth their money.

Write a letter to persuade those people. Be sure to include all the good things you think you'll bring back, and how your investors will get their money back—and more!

Today begins National School Lunch Week.

Prompt: What's the best school lunch you've ever had? What's the worst one? Can you think of three ways to make lunches at your school better?

● OCTOBER 13 ●

This day is a legal holiday in South Dakota that's known as Native Americans' Day, in honor of the great Native American leaders who contributed so much to the history of this state.

Prompt: Look up the names of some of the great Native Americans from your state. Choose one person and tell about him or her. You might wish to include a favorite story or adventure from this person's life that interests you.

Today is the first day of National Pet Peeve Week. A pet peeve is something a person finds annoying. For example, your pet peeve might be when your little brother or sister eats the last of the cookies.

Prompt: Make a list of your pet peeves. Next to each peeve, include a suggestion for how it might be changed for the better. It might also be fun to make a list of "reverse peeves," or bothersome things *you* do (like leaving the cap off the toothpaste, or forgetting to empty the trash, etc.).

● OCTOBER 14 ●

William Penn, a Quaker and the founder of Philadelphia, Pennsylvania, was born today in 1644 in London, England. On the same day in 1655, an act was passed in Massachusetts to keep out Quakers. In 1682, William Penn founded the colony of Pennsylvania as a refuge for the persecuted Quakers. In 1984, William Penn was finally declared an honorary citizen of the United States.

Prompt: How would you feel if you weren't allowed to live where you wanted to because of your beliefs? Can you name any other groups of people who came to America seeking religious freedom?

Today in 1899, The Literary Digest of New York printed the following statement about the future of automobiles:

> "At present the horseless carriage is a luxury for the wealthy; and although its price will probably fall...it will never, of course, come into as common use as the bicycle."

Prompt: What do you think would have happened to world progress if every inventor listened to commentaries like this one? If the inventor of the automobile were alive today, what do you think he would say?

● OCTOBER 15 ●

On this day in 1892, the Crow Reservation was opened for settlement. The U.S. government paid the Crow people fifty cents per acre for 1.8 million acres of their land in the mountainous western area of Montana so that settlers could live there.

Prompt: Do you think the sale was a fair one? Why or why not? If not, why do you think the Crow people agreed to the sale? What do you think they should have received in return for their land?

_____

White Cane Safety Day is celebrated today to focus our awareness on the rights and safety of the visually impaired. Blind people carry canes to help them safely find their way around obstacles. The canes are white to alert other pedestrians that the person is visually impaired.

Prompt: Describe three tasks that would be difficult for you if you were visually impaired.

⦿ OCTOBER 16 ⦿

Noah Webster, the compiler of the first American dictionary of the English language, was born today in 1758 in Hartford, Connecticut. It's no coincidence that today is also known as Dictionary Day, a day to encourage every person to own at least one dictionary and to use it every day.

Prompt: What do you think would happen if all the dictionaries in the world suddenly disappeared? How would this event affect you? Whom do you think a dictionary disappearance would bother the most?

_____

Today is the United Nations World Food Day. It was created to call attention to the shortage of food in many parts of the world, and to the fact

that even in wealthy countries like the United States, people often go hungry.

Prompt: Name three things you and your friends might do to help others on World Food Day.

⦿ OCTOBER 17 ⦿

Today in 1711, America's first published black poet, Jupiter Hammon, was born. His birth date is celebrated each year as Black Poetry Day. Mr. Hammon was born into slavery, but he was taught to read when most slaves were not allowed this privilege. His poem, "An Evening Thought," was published on Christmas Day in 1760.

Prompt: Why do you think slaves in America were not allowed to learn to read? How would you feel if you were told you weren't allowed to read?

_____

Today is International Day for the Eradication of Poverty. It was started by the United Nations to focus public awareness on the need to stop poverty and homelessness all over the world.

Prompt: How might someone your age help the poor and the homeless? What could you do on your own? What could you do as a class?

⦿ OCTOBER 18 ⦿

World Rain Forest Week begins today. This week, people will work to raise awareness of rain forest destruction. Every second, 2.4 acres of forest are destroyed. That's equal to two football fields. The forests are cleared so that builders can use the land.

Prompt: Can you think of a way to save the rain forest, but make farmers and builders happy? If not, which cause do you think is more important? Explain.

The Woolly Worm Festival is celebrated today in Banner Elk, North Carolina.

Prompt: If you could organize a festival around an insect, which bug would you choose? Give the reasons for your choice.

⊘ OCTOBER 19 ⊘

Today begins National School Bus Safety Week.

Prompt: Imagine you are a school bus driver. What three safety rules would you most want kids to observe while riding on your bus? What three things would you most want passengers *not* to do? Explain.

In 1960, today was named National Forest Products Day.

Prompt: Make a list of products we get from trees (try to include at least 5-10 products). Which of these products is most useful to you? Do you think trees should be cut down for these products? If so, how would you make sure there are enough trees left?

⊘ OCTOBER 20 ⊘

Today is the first day of National Businesswomen's Week.

Prompt: What is a businesswoman? (Give a definition of your own.) Does she have to wear a suit and work in an office, or can she be the woman who owns the local deli? Who is your favorite businesswoman? Why?

The end of hurricane season is celebrated today in the U.S. Virgin Islands as Hurricane Thanksgiving Day.

Prompt: Does your area typically have any natural disasters? Do you celebrate when they are over? What other events does your community celebrate?

⊘ OCTOBER 21 ⊘

On this day in 1772, English poet Samuel Taylor Coleridge (author of "The Rime of the Ancient Mariner" and "Kubla Khan") was born. He once wrote that "...Prose = words in their best order, and poetry = the best words in the best order."

Prompt: What do you think Coleridge means by this? Do you agree? Explain why or why not.

Dizzy Gillespie, one of the most famous jazz trumpet players of all time, was born today in 1917 in Cheraw, South Carolina. In 1953, someone fell on Dizzy's trumpet and bent it. Dizzy discovered he could hear the sound better and kept it that way. Wouldn't you know, that bent trumpet became his trademark!

Prompt: Have you (or has anyone you know) ever had something happen that at first seemed terrible, but ended up great? (For example, you were sad because you thought everyone forgot your birthday, only to have all your friends jump out and yell "surprise" as you walked into your house.)

⊘ OCTOBER 22 ⊘

Today in 1962, the U.S. faced one of its most trying times. U.S. President John F. Kennedy demanded that the U.S.S.R. (Russia) get rid of missiles in Cuba, a country in South America. The missiles were aimed at the U.S. For a while, it looked like the U.S.S.R. would refuse, and war might begin, but finally the U.S.S.R. cooperated, and the U.S. agreed to remove some missiles that were aimed at Russia.

Prompt: How do you think the people of the U.S. and the U.S.S.R. felt on that day? How do you think President Kennedy felt? If you were the President, would you have made the same demand of Russia?

Sarah Bernhardt, a famous actress in French history, was born today in 1844. Bernhardt was considered one of the greatest actresses of all time. She had a beautiful voice that seemed to capture people "like magic."

Prompt: Is there any performer (singer, actor, dancer, etc.) you've seen (either live or on television) who seems to "make magic" when you watch him or her? Describe what this person does to make you feel this way.

⊘ OCTOBER 23 ⊘

This is the traditional day for the swallows to depart each year from the old mission in San Juan Capistrano, California. This day is also the anniversary of the death of St. John of Capistrano. March 19 marks the traditional day for the swallows to return.

Prompt: How do you think the swallows know it's time to leave? (If you're not sure, make up a reason!) Can you think of any other events in nature that occur with exact timing?

Today is Television Talk Show Host Day.

Prompt: Do you watch talk shows? Why or why not? If you had your own talk show, what three people would you invite on your show? What questions would you ask your guests?

⊘ OCTOBER 24 ⊘

Today in 1901, Mrs. Anna Edson Taylor became the first person to go over Niagara Falls in a barrel—and survive. She did this foolish stunt in order to win a bet.

Prompt: How far would you go to win a bet? Think about it. Would you swim with a hungry shark? Would you sleep in a bat cave or a haunted house? How much money would be too much to pass up?

The United Nations was founded on this day in 1945, and in 1971 it became a national holiday: United Nations Day. The United Nations is a group of countries that work together to promote world peace and solve problems.

Prompt: Can you think of at least two reasons why countries need to work together?

◎ OCTOBER 25 ◎

Pablo Picasso was born today in 1881 in Malaga, Spain. He was one of the greatest artists of the 20th century. Picasso started painting realistic pictures when he was only 14. His most famous painting is *Guernica*, which he painted as a protest against the horrible bombing of the town Guernica during the Spanish Civil War. He created art until he died at the age of 92.

Prompt: Look up some of Picasso's paintings. (Your library should have some art books.) Choose one that you like and find its name. What was it about this painting that made you choose it?

Today is Cartoonists Against Crime Day; to honor cartoonists, graphic designers, and illustrators who wish to promote the prevention of crime through the art of cartooning. Their motto is, "Cartoonists Against Crime: We Draw Cartoons—Not Guns!"

Prompt: If you were asked to choose a cartoon or comic strip that promotes the thinking behind the above motto and slogan, which one would you choose? Give the reasons for your choice.

◎ OCTOBER 26 ◎

Author Steven Kellogg (*Pecos Bill* and *Johnny Appleseed*) was born today in 1941 in Norwalk, Connecticut. Steven says that when he was a kid he knew many adults who hated their jobs, so when he goes into schools he tells students: "It's important to know yourself as well as you can, because then you can choose the job and lifestyle that's right for you."

Prompt: Name two jobs you might like to have when you're older. What made you choose these particular jobs?

Today in 1369, the King of France, Charles V (also known as "Charles the Wise"), dedicated a monument to his personal chef, Benkels, for inventing a recipe for pickled fish that delighted the King.

Prompt: If you could dedicate a monument to anyone for any reason, whom would you choose? For what reason? Describe what the monument would look like, and where you'd have it placed.

⊘ OCTOBER 27 ⊘

Theodore Roosevelt, the 26th President of the U.S., was born today in 1858 in New York City. He was the first President to ever ride in an automobile (1902) or fly in an airplane (1910). He once said, "The first requisite [requirement] of a good citizen in this Republic of ours is that he shall be able and willing to pull his weight."

Prompt: Explain what you think Theodore Roosevelt meant by his definition of a good citizen. How might this definition apply to someone your age? Make up your own definition for a "good citizen."

———

Today is Navy Day; it has been celebrated since 1922.

Prompt: Can you name all four main branches of our armed forces? Do you have a favorite branch? Choose one, and name three ways you might celebrate its day. Do you think you might enlist someday? Explain why or why not.

⊘ OCTOBER 28 ⊘

On this day in 1886, Frederic Auguste Bartholdi's famous sculpture *Liberty Enlightening the World* was dedicated in New York Harbor. This sculpture was a gift from France to the United States, and became known around the world as the Statue of Liberty. A 1903 poem by Emma Lazarus was inscribed on its pedestal.

Prompt: Imagine you are an immigrant coming to this country in search of a better life. You see the Statue of Liberty for the first time. Pretend you are writing about this moment in a diary. What would you say? If you need help getting started, describe what you see: other immigrants, the statue, sunlight, etc. Then tell how these things make you feel.

———

Today is Saint Jude's Day, in honor of the Roman Catholic Saint of hopeless causes. St. Jude is very popular with those who wish to accomplish something very difficult.

Prompt: If you had the power to grant three wishes that would solve three hopeless causes, name the "wishes" you would grant.

⊘ OCTOBER 29 ⊘

When you hear of "Black Tuesday," think of the great Stock Market Crash of 1929, which sent America into its greatest depression (a time when many people are out of work because the economy, or how much each dollar is really worth, is in very bad shape). The Great Depression lasted for 10 years and involved North America, Europe, and other countries that depended upon industry (factory-produced goods).

Prompt: Why do you think this time in American history is called "The Great Depression"?

———

Daniel Decatur Emmett, the composer of "Dixie" (the fighting song for the Confederate troops during the Civil War), was born today in 1815 in Mount Vernon, Ohio. "Dixie" is still the unofficial anthem of the South.

Prompt: Why do you think music becomes so important to men and women during wartime? If you had to leave your family and go to war, and could only take one song (or album) with you, which one would you take? Give the reasons for your choice.

◎ OCTOBER 30 ◎

John Adams, second President of the United States (he had been George Washington's Vice President) and the father of John Quincy Adams (who became the sixth President of the U.S.), was born today in 1735 in Braintree, Massachusetts. He died on July 4, 1826, on the 50th anniversary of the adoption of the Declaration of Independence.

Prompt: John Adams and John Quincy Adams are the only father and son to both share the Presidency. Why do you think it might be difficult to become President after your father has already held that office successfully? If you could follow in anyone's footstep's (it need not be a family member), whose would you choose? Give your reasons.

Emily Post, newspaper columnist and expert on manners, was born today in 1872 in Baltimore, Maryland. Post's book, *Etiquette*, had already been published ten times at the time of her death at age 87.

Prompt: What do you consider good manners? Explain what you consider the three most important rules of etiquette. (Saying "thank you"? Covering your mouth when you sneeze?)

◎ OCTOBER 31 ◎

This was the day in 1941 that the *Mount Rushmore National Memorial* was completed. It took 14 years of work to finish the 60-foot sculpture of the heads of four Presidents: George Washington (who stood for the nation's *founding*), Thomas Jefferson (who stood for its *political philosophy*), Abraham Lincoln (who stood for its *preservation*), and Theodore Roosevelt (who stood for its *expansion and conservation*).

Prompt: Read more about one of the above Presidents and give at least one reason why you think he was chosen to stand for the quality listed after him.

Harry Houdini, the famous magician and escape artist, died today in 1926 in Detroit, Michigan. In his honor, today is also known as National Magic Day.

Prompt: Have you ever watched a magician perform? Do you have a favorite magic trick? Describe it. Which do you think you'd prefer: performing a magic trick or watching one?

NOVEMBER

November is National Creative Child Month dating back to the first aeronautical experiments performed in 1782 by French brothers Joseph and Michael Montgolfier. The brothers tried filling paper and fabric bags with smoke and hot air, which lead to the invention of hot air balloons and the first flight. Imagine, a backyard experiment lead mankind into flight!

Prompt: Have you ever heard of any other discoveries in the scientific world that began with a simple experiment—or even an accident? Think about discoveries in weather, medicine, industry, etc. Did *you* (or anyone you know) ever invent or discover something useful by accident?

NOVEMBER 1

Each year around this time, thousands of runners gather in New York City to compete in the world-famous New York City Marathon. Millions of spectators watch this famous race from the sidelines.

Prompt: If you had the chance to run in this famous marathon, would you do it? How would you prepare? If you could choose, what major sports event would you take part in? The World Series? Super Bowl? Olympics? Explain.

Today in 1990, McDonald's Corporation stopped its use of polystyrene plastic-foam containers and started using paper containers.

Prompt: Why do you think McDonald's made this decision? If you were in charge of McDonald's Corporation, would you make any other changes (in the menu, service, packaging, decor, etc.)? Give your reasons.

NOVEMBER 2

Daniel Boone's birthday is today. He was born in Berks County, Pennsylvania, in 1734. He led a rugged, interesting life. He was captured by the Shawnee Indians in 1778 and adopted by the tribe as "Big Turtle." He was then captured by the British in 1781. He died in 1820.

Prompt: Native Americans often select names from nature. The Shawnee might have called Daniel Boone "Big Turtle" because he was slow, like a turtle. Or maybe he was shy (think about what a turtle does when you frighten it). If you were given a Native American name, what might it be? Explain why.

Today begins National Split Pea Soup Week.

Prompt: What is your favorite soup? Do you like this soup enough to eat it for a whole week? If not, what food would you consider worthy of your attention for an entire week?

⊘ NOVEMBER 3 ⊘

Today in 1938 in Shanghai, China, Bette Bao Lord, the author of *In the Year of the Boar and Jackie Robinson*, was born. For anyone wishing to write, Bette's best advice comes in one word: "Start." Her own experience has proven that the first sentence is the most difficult because: "It seems to set the tone or get you ready to go."

Prompt: Do you agree with Bette Bao Lord, that the first sentence of any writing project is always the most difficult? What do you do when you have a hard time with that first sentence?

Today is Sandwich Day, in honor of John Montagu, Fourth Earl of Sandwich, who was born today in 1718. The Earl did not invent the sandwich, but he sure did make it popular. He ate sandwiches all the time as a time-saving way to dine while he was gambling. (One session lasted 24 hours!)

Prompt: When you want to save time, yet are hungry, what do you eat? If it's a sandwich, what kind is it?

⊘ NOVEMBER 4 ⊘

Around this time of year, you might start to see stores decorating for Christmas, Hanukkah, and other winter holidays. Stores also start putting a lot of advertisements on TV and in newspapers. Why? They want people to buy, buy, buy!

Prompt: Did you ever buy a toy or other product after seeing it in an advertisement? Were you happy with the product or disappointed? Explain.

The first Tuesday in November is Election Day in our country.

Prompt: Imagine you are running for mayor of your city or town. Name three things you would promise to do as mayor? How would you win people's trust—and votes?

⊘ NOVEMBER 5 ⊘

Thomas Sully died today in Philadelphia, Pennsylvania, in 1872. Sully painted nearly 2,000 portraits of people in his time. He also painted his re-creation of nearly 500 historical subjects, including the famous painting *Washington Crossing the Delaware*.

Prompt: Besides paintings, how do we know about history? How do you think an event like Washington crossing the Delaware would be recorded for history today?

Today begins the Canadian Finals Rodeo, held annually in Edmonton Coliseum in Western Canada. It features the top-ten winners in each of six rodeo events: Bull Riding, Bareback

Riding, Saddle Bronc Riding, Calf Roping, Steer Wrestling, and Ladies Barrel Racing.

Prompt: If you were asked to compete in one of the above events, which one would you definitely *not* choose? Give the reasons for your choice. Which would you choose, instead? (No experience necessary!)

⊘ NOVEMBER 6 ⊘

Baseball's World Series is over, and people are paying more attention to basketball and other winter sports.

Prompt: Baseball is often called America's national pastime. Do you think baseball should continue to hold this honor? Why or why not? If not, which sport do you think should be America's favorite sport?

James Naismith, the inventor of the game of basketball, was born today in Altamonte, Ontario, Canada, in 1861. Little did he know that basketball would become an Olympic sport in 1936.

Prompt: Why do you think basketball is such a popular sport? Imagine you were the inventor of this game. Create the scene that led you to its invention. (Use your imagination and don't be afraid to be funny; for example, do you think the first basketball was really a ball?)

⊘ NOVEMBER 7 ⊘

On this day in 1944, Franklin D. Roosevelt became the first (and only) person to ever be elected to a fourth term (each term is four years) as President of the United States. He died in office, after serving only 53 days of this term.

Prompt: Do you think it's a good idea to allow one person to serve so many terms as President (or as any other public official)? Name two advantages and two disadvantages of having one leader serve for so long?

The symbol for the Republican Party (the elephant), first appeared today in 1874, in a cartoon in the magazine Harper's Weekly. The elephant symbolized the Republican Party because the party was so big. Later, a donkey was used to represent the Democrats. Many people thought President Andrew Jackson, a Democrat, was as foolish as a donkey!

Prompt: If you were asked to start a new political party in America, what would you call it? What symbol would you choose to stand for this new party? Remember, a symbol can be an animal, something from nature, a design, or an object that reminds people of the thing it stands for.

NOVEMBER 8

Edmund Halley, the astronomer/mathematician who discovered Halley's Comet, was born today in London, England, in 1656. Halley's Comet appears about every 76 years, so that once a generation, Edmund is remembered.

Prompt: If you could have something in nature (a star, a forest, a mountain, a planet, etc.) named after you, what would you choose? Why?

The x-ray was invented today in 1895 by physicist Wilhelm Conrad Roentgen.

Prompt: Have you ever been x-rayed? Name at least one way you think the practice of medicine has improved because of this discovery. Then list three other inventions in the field of medicine that you think are important.

NOVEMBER 9

Today in 1955 in Jackson, Michigan, the National Child Safety Council was founded.

Prompt: Based on your experience, what do you think are the three most important safety tips for kids? Why?

The *Vietnam Veterans Memorial* was unveiled today in 1984. This memorial contains the statue *Three Servicemen* (sculpted by Frederick Hart), which faces a black granite wall where the names of more than 58,000 Americans who were killed or missing in action during the Vietnam War are inscribed.

Prompt: Have you ever visited this memorial? Share your experience. What feelings do you think a war veteran might have when he or she sees the memorial?

NOVEMBER 10

The television show *Sesame Street* had its first episode today in 1969.

Prompt: Who is your favorite Muppet character on Sesame Street? Kermit? Big Bird? Oscar? Elmo? Ernie or Bert? What do you like most about this character?

Tomorrow is Veterans' Day, a time to remember all the people in the Armed Forces who have served our country.

Prompt: Write a letter to a veteran (it might be a person you know well or someone in your community). In your letter, thank the veteran for all the positive actions he or she has taken to protect our nation. Tomorrow, share a copy of your letter with that person.

NOVEMBER 11

Abigail Adams, First Lady to John Adams, the second President of the U.S., was born today in Weymouth, Massachusetts, in 1744. Not every First Lady builds a reputation in her own right, but Abigail certainly did. She was renowned as a gracious hostess to national and world leaders.

Prompt: Can you think of any other First Lady whom you admire? Give your reason for choosing her.

The song "God Bless America," written by Irving Berlin, was first performed today in 1938 by Kate Smith. The song was written especially for Smith.

Prompt: Have you ever sung this song? Some people like it better than the "Star-Spangled Banner" and think it should become our new national anthem. What do you think?

⊘ NOVEMBER 12 ⊘

On this day in 1892, William "Pudge" Heffelfinger was paid a cash bonus of $500 (in addition to a whopping $25 for expenses) to become the first professional football player.

Prompt: Today, football players and other sports stars earn millions of dollars each year. On the other hand, teachers often earn less than $50,000, while the President earns about $200,000 a year. Some people argue that sports stars' salaries are fair because the players entertain the whole country. Do *you* think professional sports salaries are too high? Why or why not?

Elizabeth Cady Stanton, champion of women's rights, was born today in 1815 in Johnstown, New York. At the first Women's Rights Convention in 1848, Stanton said, "We hold these truths to be self-evident, that all men and women are created equal."

Prompt: When he wrote the Gettysburg Address, Abraham Lincoln was the first person to ever begin a speech with, "We hold these truths to be self-evident...." Look up Lincoln's famous speech, then compare its first line to Elizabeth Cady Stanton's. What's different? Why do you think Stanton made this change?

⊘ NOVEMBER 13 ⊘

In 1967, Carl Burton Stokes became the first African-American in the United States to be elected mayor. The city he governed was Cleveland, Ohio.

Prompt: Why do you think it took so long for an African-American to be elected mayor of a U.S. city? Can you think of any other African-Americans today who are prominent politicians?

Today in 1927, the Holland Tunnel opened. The tunnel is under the Hudson River; it connects New York City to New Jersey. The first underwater tunnel ever built, it is still used each day by hundreds of thousands of people.

Prompt: How do you think an underwater tunnel is built? Would you have wanted to be one of the first people to drive in the tunnel?

⊘ NOVEMBER 14 ⊘

Nelly Bly (a fake name used by newspaper reporter Elizabeth Cochrane Seaman) started a journey around the world on this day in 1889. She hoped to beat the imaginary record set by Phileas Fogg in the book *Around the World in Eighty Days* by Jules Verne. And Nelly Bly succeeded. She made her trip in just 72 days, 6 hours, and 14 seconds.

Prompt: Have you ever wanted to set a world record (and maybe even make it into the *Guinness Book of Records*)? Tell about a record you'd like to beat. Hint: You could check out the *Guinness Book of Records* for ideas.

Get ready for National Children's Book Week! It's just a few days away. It's a great time to read some new books and reread your old favorites.

Prompt: What is your favorite "old" book? What is your favorite "new" book? Give two reasons why you like each one.

NOVEMBER 15

Shichi-Go-San, a children's festival, is celebrated today in Japan. Shichi-Go-San means the "Seven-Five-Three" rite where parents take all 3-year-old children (boys and girls), all 5-year-old boys, and all 7-year-old girls—dressed in their best clothes—to a Shinto shrine. Here, parents pray their children will grow up healthy and free from worries. Then it's time for a party complete with presents, games, and candy.

Prompt: Make up a children's festival of your own involving both parents and children. Include how people should dress, where they would go, what activities are planned. And don't forget to plan the party. (If there is one, of course!)

Today is the birthday of Georgia O'Keeffe, one of the greatest American artists of the 20th century. She was born in Sun Prairie, Wyoming, in 1887 and later painted images from these surroundings, such as prairie flowers. One of her works, *Summer Days*, sold to designer Calvin Klein for $1 million. O'Keeffe died in 1986 at the age of 98.

Prompt: Do you have a favorite painter? Would you pay $1 million for one of his or her paintings (if you had the money)? If you don't have a favorite painter, look in a book of art and choose a painting! Then tell why you chose this particular work of art.

NOVEMBER 16

Children's author Jean Fritz was born today in 1915 in Hankow, China, where she spent her first twelve years. Fritz wanted very badly to live in America (where her parents were from), and she grew up with a deep feeling for U.S. history. This interest influenced her writing; she wrote many biographies about America's founders and its early history (*Why Don't You Get a Horse, Sam Adams?*, and *Bully for You, Teddy Roosevelt!*, etc.). She once commented: "No one is more patriotic than the one separated from his or her country...No one is as eager to find roots as the person who has been uprooted."

Prompt: Do you feel uprooted from your country? If not, do you know anyone who might feel uprooted? Explain how it might feel to be living in a different country than where you were born—or think of a kind act you can do to make someone who is uprooted feel better.

November 16 begins National Education Week.

Prompt: Think about your school and your classroom. Make a list of at least three things you would do to improve education from your point of view. For example, would you include more books in the library? Would you include music lessons every day?

❍ NOVEMBER 17 ❍

The formal opening of the Suez Canal happened today in 1869 in Egypt. The Suez Canal is a waterway that shortens the route between England and India by 6,000 miles. The canal itself is about 100 miles long and joins the Mediterranean and Red seas.

Prompt: Look up the Suez Canal on a map. Can you see why it saves a sea journey of 6,000 miles? Now think about your own everyday travels. Do you use a shortcut? Where might you create a shortcut to make your trips faster and easier?

Today is Isamu Noguchi's birthday. He is an American sculptor who was born in Los Angeles in 1904. Noguchi's work is abstract (it doesn't have a recognizable subject). Noguchi has designed settings for ballets, furniture, and has even worked with architects to plan gardens, playgrounds, and bridges.

Prompt: If you could design a sculpture for your playground, what would it look like? What would it be made of? (Remember, a person can make a sculpture from *any* material he or she wishes.)

❍ NOVEMBER 18 ❍

South Africa adopted a new constitution today in 1993. After more than 300 years of white rulership, basic civil rights (the right to vote, freedom of speech, etc.) were finally granted to black people in South Africa.

Prompt: If you were creating a constitution (set of basic laws) for a new country, name the first three laws you would impose. Which law do you consider the most important?

Beginning today in 1870, English mail was delivered to France by carrier pigeon.

Prompt: Why do you think mail delivery by pigeons was a good idea in 1870? Compare that method with the methods you use to send mail today.

❍ NOVEMBER 19 ❍

Get out your globes! This week is National Geography Awareness Week.

Prompt: Where in the world would you most like to visit? Why? Where would you most like to live?

Today in 1653 in London, England, a local newspaper reported that the current fashion trend among women was to put fake moles and tiny cutouts of planets and stars all over their faces.

Prompt: What's the weirdest fashion trend you've ever seen?

⟁ NOVEMBER 20 ⟁

American astronomer Edwin Hubble was born today in Marshfield, Missouri, in 1889. The Hubble Space Telescope is named for Edwin. This telescope allows people to see further into space than ever before.

Prompt: Would you like a career in space science? Why or why not? What questions would you need to have answered before making your decision?

Every year around this time, the American Cancer Society sponsors the Great American Smokeout to encourage a smoke-free environment.

Prompt: Is there anyone you'd like to encourage to stop smoking? (If you have tried smoking, you might choose yourself.) Write down the words you'd like to say to this person, then practice. If you do not know any smokers, write a letter to someone your own age urging them never to start smoking.

⟁ NOVEMBER 21 ⟁

Children's author Elizabeth George Speare was born today in 1908 in Melrose, Massachusetts. She has made history come alive for children in novels such as *The Bronze Bow*, and *The Sign of*

the Beaver. She confesses: "In my school days I was never very fond of history."

Prompt: Why do you suppose Elizabeth Speare changed her mind about history? Can you think of a book you've read that made history come alive for you?

Hetty Green (Henrietta Robinson Green), was considered one of the richest women in America in the late 1800s. She managed her own money—something very few women did back then. Today is her birthday.

Prompt: Fill in the blanks with what *you* would most like to be remembered as. Then explain why!

The _____ woman/man in _____.

⟁ NOVEMBER 22 ⟁

National Stop the Violence Day has been celebrated each year since 1990. November 22 was chosen in honor of President John F. Kennedy, who was a victim of violence on this day in 1963. On National Stop the Violence Day, people wear white ribbons and drive with car headlights on as a show of peace.

Prompt: Do you know of anyone who has been hurt or killed due to an act of violence? (It could be someone famous.) What would you like to say to people who commit such crimes?

Around this time every year, a giant tree is cut down and moved to a famous spot in New York City: Rockefeller Center. There, the tree is decorated with Christmas lights.

Thousands of people come every year to see the tree.

Prompt: Some people argue that trees shouldn't be cut down just for decoration. Others say a Christmas tree is an important tradition for many families. Which side do you agree with? Why? Can you think of a way to make both sides happy?

✪ NOVEMBER 23 ✪

Today begins National Adoption Week, to celebrate families with adopted kids. About one out of every 63 children in the U.S. are adopted. Note: Some famous people who came to their families through adoption are: Presidents Herbert Hoover and Gerald Ford, Nancy Reagan, Dave Thomas (founder of "Wendy's"), and Scott Hamilton (ice skating champ).

Prompt: Loving and caring for a child is what makes a real parent. Name three ways you might show these qualities to your child—if you were a parent.

The last week in November is National Game and Puzzle Week. Why not spend some time with family and friends playing games?

Prompt: Describe your favorite game. Is it a board game? A game you play outdoors? Use your imagination to think up a new game you could play with friends.

✪ NOVEMBER 24 ✪

Born today in Texarkana, Texas, was the prize-winning African-American pianist and composer, Scott Joplin. His "Maple Leaf Rag" (published in 1899) was the first piece of sheet music to sell more than 1 million copies! Scott was born in 1868, and when he was composing in the 1800s, some people called his music poison.

Prompt: Have you ever heard any of Scott Joplin's music? If so, what do you think of it? If a grown-up ever criticized the music you like to listen to, what would you say?

Today we celebrate the birthday of children's author Gloria Houston, who has written *My Great-Aunt Arizona*, *But No Candy*, and other books. The books are based on family stories Houston grew up hearing in the Appalachian Mountains. She hopes her books encourage children to value their families.

Prompt: Do you know any family stories? Write your story down. If you don't know one, write about something that has happened to you that you would want to share with your children and grandchildren.

✪ NOVEMBER 25 ✪

Author/illustrator Marc Brown was born today in 1946 in Erie, Pennsylvania. Marc is well known for his character "Arthur." But the book he's proudest of is *Dinosaurs Divorce*, which he hopes helps children talk about how they feel when parents split up.

Prompt: Have you or has anyone you know been affected by a divorce? What do you think are the three biggest feelings a child experiences when his or her parents get divorced? Can you think of any ways you might be helpful to a friend if divorce is happening in his or her family?

Andrew Carnegie, an American businessman who was famous for his great wealth, was born today in Scotland in 1835. Carnegie believed that rich people should use their extra money to help their communities. Carnegie was true to his word. He paid for the building of more than 2,500 libraries and regularly donated money to charities.

Prompt: If you were wealthy, would you give away some (or all) of your money? If so, name three ways you would share your money with others.

⊘ NOVEMBER 26 ⊘

On this day in 1789, George Washington proclaimed November 26 Thanksgiving Day. He and U.S. lawmakers set aside the day to be thankful for our country and our government. Today, our traditional Thanksgiving Day is celebrated on the fourth Thursday in November.

Prompt: There are plenty of things to be thankful for every day of the year. Do you think having a public holiday as a reminder is a good idea? Name the three things you are thankful for *every day*.

In Wichita, Kansas, people are encouraged to consider this day *What Do You Love About America Day*, and to talk about why they enjoy living in the U.S.

Prompt: Think carefully, then choose three things you *love* about America. Give your reasons for each choice.

⊘ NOVEMBER 27 ⊘

The day after Thanksgiving is often called Black Friday. Why? Many people start their holiday shopping on this day. They spend lots of money, helping stores move their accounting books from the "red" (losing money) to the "black" (making a profit).

Prompt: You may not want to brave the crowds on Black Friday, but you could start a holiday gift list for your family and friends. Think up a dream gift for five people on your list.

Anders Celsius, a Swedish astronomer and inventor, was born today in 1701. He invented the thermometer and developed the Celsius scale of measurement, in which 0 degrees marks the freezing point and 100 degrees is boiling.

Prompt: If you could have an invention named after you, what would it be? (It's OK if it's already been invented.)

⊘ NOVEMBER 28 ⊘

William Blake, an English poet and artist, was born today in 1757 in London, England. He believed that many people were too greedy for "things." This idea shows up frequently in Blake's work.

Prompt: Do you agree or disagree with William Blake's idea that people put too much value on the wrong things? Give an example of some "wrong things" that you think people value. Make a list of things in your life that you think are valuable, yet don't cost any money. Note: If you wish to further explore the poems of William Blake, see Nancy Willard's book for children: *A Visit to William Blake's Inn.*

___

Fish House Parade happens today in Aitkin, Minnesota. The little houses that fishermen use for ice fishing in the winter (you might have seen these fish houses in the movie *Grumpy Old Men*) are creatively decorated for a parade.

Prompt: Can you think of any other cold weather events that might be celebrated during the winter months?

⊘ NOVEMBER 29 ⊘

Today in 1832 in Philadelphia, Pennsylvania, Louisa May Alcott, the author of the children's novel *Little Women*, was born. When she was ten years old, Louisa wrote in her diary: "I wish I was rich, I was good, and we were all a happy family this day."

Prompt: Have you ever felt the way Louisa May Alcott was feeling the day she wrote this in her diary? Louisa probably felt better after she wrote for a while. What makes you feel better when you're feeling blue?

___

Charles Thomson, America's first, official record keeper, was born today in Ireland in 1729. He was the chosen secretary for the First Continental Congress (the lawmaking group that is now the U.S. Congress), and recorded all of its meetings for 15 years.

Prompt: Name at least three kinds of records your teacher must keep. How about your parents?

⊘ NOVEMBER 30 ⊘

Achoo! Cold and flu season is here. Some people think cold weather makes people sick, but that's not true. Actually, cold weather simply forces people inside, where germs can spread around more easily.

Prompt: Think of a time you were sick with a cold or flu. Describe your sick feelings with colors; for example, "My stomach felt lime green." Explain why you chose each color.

___

The first Sunday after Thanksgiving is a special day in Pasadena, California. An event called the Pasadena Doo Dah Parade happens every year. The Doo Dah Parade prides itself on having no theme, no prizes, no order for marchers, no motorized vehicles, and no animals!

Prompt: What do you imagine this parade looks like? Do you think it's a good idea? If you were asked to be in this parade, how would you go about it?

December has been designated as National Stress-Free Family Holidays Month.

Prompt: Does your family sometimes stress out at holiday time? What could you do to make these times less stressful for everyone?

DECEMBER 1

Today is Rosa Parks Day. It marks the anniversary of Parks's 1955 arrest in Montgomery, Alabama, for refusing to give up her front seat on a bus to a white passenger. Her bravery in the face of violent hatred is often called the birth of the Civil Rights Movement. Her arrest led to lawsuits which ended racial segregation on city buses all over the southern United States.

Prompt: Can you imagine how you would feel if someone said that you (or your mother or father or grandparents, etc.) were not good enough to ride in the front of a bus or train? Can you believe that some people still feel this way? What would you say if someone acted in this unkind manner in front of you?

December 1 begins Deaf Heritage Week. We specifically remember Laurent Clerk and Thomas Hopkins Gallaudet, pioneers in education for the deaf in the U.S.

Prompt: Do you know anyone who is hearing-impaired? In addition to sign language, how could people communicate without being able to speak or hear?

DECEMBER 2

December 2, 1982, marked the first artificial heart transplant. The surgery was successfully performed on a 61-year-old man named Barney Clark at the University of Utah Medical Center in Salt Lake City. He survived for 112 days. (Dr. Christian Barnard, a South African surgeon, performed the first successful real heart transplant in 1967).

Prompt: How do you think people reacted when doctors first announced they wanted to put an artificial heart in a person?

Today is National Roof-Over-Your-Head Day, to focus public attention on ways to help the homeless all over America.

Prompt: What are some of the things homeless people probably have to do without? Describe some different ways you might help the homeless in your community. (Hint: What "gifts" do you have that you might share—toys, clothing?)

◊ DECEMBER 3 ◊

Today marks the United Nations resolution to make December 3 International Day of Disabled Persons, to help make it easier for disabled people all over the world to function better in public places.

Prompt: Name something your school does to make life easier for disabled people. Name something you could do. What would you say to someone who *isn't* disabled, yet insists on using special parking spaces set aside for people who truly need them?

Happy birthday, Anna Chlomsky! Anna is the actress who starred in the hit movie *My Girl*. She was born today in 1980.

Prompt: What do you think it is like to be a child star? Do you think it is always fun? Explain.

◊ DECEMBER 4 ◊

Today begins Wild About Wildlife month at the Coastal Center for the Arts in St. Simons Island, Georgia.

Prompt: Think of an animal you're "wild" about, and explain why you chose this creature. Have you ever tried to draw, paint, or photograph this species?

Day of the Artisans is celebrated on this day to honor the nation's workers.

Prompt: Workers help a community run. They do everything from keeping our heaters running in winter to stocking boxes of food at the grocery store. Is there a worker you'd like to honor today? Explain what this person does each day, and the importance of his or her job.

◊ DECEMBER 5 ◊

Born today in Salzburg, Austria, in 1756 was the man some people regard as the greatest musical genius of all time: Wolfgang Amadeus Mozart. Mozart began composing his own pieces at age 5, and toured Europe as a concert pianist at age 6. Although he composed numerous piano works and operas like *Don Giovanni* and *The Magic Flute* for both an Archbishop and an Emperor, Mozart constantly had to borrow money to live. He died penniless in 1791 at the age of 35.

Prompt: Can you imagine being so famous at such a young age? Have you ever heard any of Mozart's music? If not, borrow a tape or CD from your local library. Which piece is your favorite? Why?

Theodore Roosevelt wrote to his son Kermit today in 1906, explaining why he was refusing the money (about $40,000) that went with his Nobel Peace Prize award: "...I could not accept any money given to me for making peace between two nations, especially when I was able to make peace simply because I was President..."

Prompt: What do you think of President Roosevelt's refusal to accept money for helping countries make peace? If you were the President, would you have done the same thing? Why or why not?

DECEMBER 6

Today in 1877, Thomas Alva Edison made the first sound recording into a phonograph that he designed. He recited "Mary had a little lamb..."

Prompt: If you were about to make the first sound recording in history, what would you recite (or say)?

The Chester Greenwood Day Parade happens today in Farmington, Maine, in honor of the famous inventor of earmuffs who came from Farmington. The theme of the parade? Earmuffs, of course!

Prompt: Are there any famous people from your town? (It might be an inventor or a baseball player or a retired general.) If you can't think of anyone from your town, how about someone from your state? If you could be famous for inventing any little doodad or gadget in the world, which one would it be? Why?

DECEMBER 7

Today at 7:55 a.m. in 1941, Pearl Harbor (in Hawaii) was attacked by nearly 200 Japanese aircraft. The air attack destroyed much of the U.S. Pacific Fleet and killed more than 3,000 people. President Franklin D. Roosevelt asked Congress to declare war on Japan, and the United States officially entered World War II. In a famous speech, President Roosevelt called December 7 "...a date that will live in infamy."

Prompt: Is there any news event from the past few years that will stick in your mind even when you're old? What made this happening so upsetting or memorable for you?

Today in 1787, Delaware became the first state to ratify, or sign, the brand-new U.S. Constitution.

Prompt: Imagine it is the year 1787, and you are sent by your state to check out the newly written Constitution. It is up to you whether or not to approve the set of laws. What kinds of laws would you want to see in the Constitution?

DECEMBER 8

Painter Diego Rivera was born today in 1886 in Guanajuato, Mexico. If you were to visit Mexico, you would probably see one of his bold-colored murals, because Rivera painted them on buildings all over the country. He tried to paint the hardships of the common people, whom he felt were mistreated by the government. Rivera's art was so convincing that the government tried to kick him out of the country.

Prompt: Have you ever learned something you didn't know from a work of art (a drawing, photograph, or mural)? Do you think it is true that "a picture is worth a thousand words"?

Today, many magazines run a list of famous people chosen as Most Boring Celebrities of the Year.

Prompt: Make up your own list of "boring" celebrities (include at least three people), then explain why you chose them.

⊘ DECEMBER 9 ⊘

Joan Blos, the author of A *Gathering of Days: A New England Girl's Journal, 1830-32,* was born today in 1928 in New York City. Joan believes you can learn a lot about life from a book, so she spends a lot of time researching her characters: their tools, their clothes and furnishings, their houses and towns, the way they talked, etc. She wants her readers to feel as if they are really there.

Prompt: Think of a book you've read that taught you something about life and/or made you feel as if you were really there. Which part of the book was your favorite? Why?

Noah Webster established *The American Minerva,* New York's first daily newspaper, today in 1793, with the following promise for what his paper would be: "The Friend of Government, of Freedom, of Virtue, and every Species of Improvement."

Prompt: What do you think the purpose of a newspaper should be? If you were a reporter for your school newspaper, what would your first story be about? BONUS: What else is Noah Webster famous for?

⊘ DECEMBER 10 ⊘

Emily Dickinson, one of America's greatest poets, was born today in 1830 in Amherst, Massachussetts. Because Dickinson was shy, very few people read her poems until after her death. She had a particular way of telling if a poem was special: "If I feel physically as if the top of my head were taken off, I know *that* is poetry," Dickinson once said.

Prompt: Have you ever felt the way Dickinson felt while reading a terrific poem or story? Do you know anyone who is private and shy like Emily was, and has a special interest or talent no one else knows about?

The Nobel Peace Prizes are awarded each year on this day to people who have made the most valuable contributions to the good of humanity. The ceremonies are held on the anniversary of Alfred Nobel's death. Nobel was the Swedish chemist (and inventor of dynamite) after whom the awards were named. The Prize is worth about $200,000.

Prompt: If you were to award a peace prize to anyone in your school, whom would you choose? Give the reasons for your choice.

DECEMBER 11

Today in 1936, King Edward VIII of England gave up being king in order to marry his true love, Wallis Warfield Simpson. The problem? Simpson was American and divorced, two strikes against her in the minds of British royalty. Edward's decision to marry Simpson caused a great scandal; all the world gossiped about his choice "for the woman I love."

Prompt: If you had the choice of being king or queen of a country or finding happiness with the person you love, which would you choose? Give the reasons for your answer.

On this day in 1844, nitrous oxide, also known as "laughing gas," was first used to numb the pain of a tooth extraction.

Prompt: Do you think you would like to be a dentist? Why or why not?

DECEMBER 12

This week in 1946, the United Nations set up a special committee called UNICEF (United Nations Children's Fund) to work for the health and well-being of children in developing countries. UNICEF workers provide food, clean water, and medicine to kids all over the world.

Prompt: If you worked for UNICEF, where would you go first? What's the first thing you would do there?

Today in 1989, Leona Helmsley, a U.S. billionaire, was fined $7 million and sentenced to four years in prison today for tax evasion. Taxes are the money people pay to the government for building roads, helping the poor, paying for public schools, etc. Tax evasion is when people break the law by not paying their taxes.

Prompt: Because Leona Helmsley earned so much money and still tried to get away without paying taxes, she was given the nickname "Queen of Greed." Do you think this nickname suits her? Why or why not? Why do you think someone so rich (who could easily afford it) didn't want to pay her taxes?

DECEMBER 13

Today is Santa Lucia Day in Sweden, where people are having a nation-wide celebration of light to honor St. Lucia. Hotels and inns have their own "Lucias," young girls dressed in long, flowing white gowns, to serve guests coffee and buns early in the morning.

Prompt: Do you take part in a holiday tradition at your house? Describe your tradition.

Today in 1917, violinist Yehudi Menuhin played for the first time at the famous Carnegie Hall in New York City. He was only ten years old! After the concert, when the audience wanted to flock around him, he just wanted ice cream.

Prompt: Some child stars become spoiled, while others do not. What do you think makes the difference? Would you want your child to be famous?

DECEMBER 14

Today begins Tell Someone They're Doing a Good Job Week. To celebrate this week properly, you must tell a different person every day that he or she is doing a good job.

Prompt: Start planning now! Choose at least four people you'd like to tell, "You're doing a good job!" Jot down their names and some reasons each person should be congratulated.

George Washington, our first President, died today in 1799.

Prompt: Imagine you were asked to deliver the eulogy, or speech, at George Washington's funeral. What would you say?

DECEMBER 15

Alexandre Gustave Eiffel, the French engineer who designed the 1,000-foot Eiffel Tower, was born today in France in 1832. (He also helped design the Statue of Liberty.)

Prompt: What is your favorite landmark? Tell why you like it.

The Bill of Rights is the list of rights given to all Americans under the U.S. Constitution. The Bill was ratified, or passed, today in 1791. The rights include:

- the right to free speech and press (you can say or write about just about anything you want);
- the right to practice whatever religion you choose;
- the right to own weapons;
- the right to a quick, fair trial if you are arrested for a crime.

Prompt: Which of the above rights do you think is most important? Why?

⊘ DECEMBER 16 ⊘

The Boston Tea Party happened today in 1773. The American colonists were angry at having to pay tax money to England (who ruled America at the time). That's because the colonists didn't have any say in how their tax money was spent. One day the English told the colonists there would be still another tax—on tea. Soon after, a crowd of more than 7,000 people dumped 342 chests of tea into the Boston harbor as a sign of rebellion.

Prompt: If you had been at the Boston "Tea Party," and been asked for your opinion on the new tax, what do you think you would have said? Why do you think this event was so important in American history?

Ludwig van Beethoven was born today in 1770 in Bonn, Germany. Considered by many to be the greatest composer ever, Beethoven became hearing impaired at age 30. But this didn't stop him; neither did becoming totally deaf! He continued to compose and perform until his death in 1827.

Prompt: Can you think of any other hearing impaired or disabled individuals who went on with their lives and accomplishments in spite of their disabilities?

⊘ DECEMBER 17 ⊘

Today is Wright Brothers' Day, in honor of Wilbur and Orville's first flight in 1903 at Kill Devil Hill, North Carolina. This flight proved that heavier-than-air flight was possible. It lasted 12 seconds at an altitude of 10 feet.

Prompt: Did you ever wish you could fly? Why? This wish prompted the Wright brothers to experiment with flight. Do you have any other "wishes" that seem impossible?

American poet John Greenleaf Whittier was born today in 1807 in Haverhill, Massachusetts. He once wrote:

For all sad words of tongue or pen,
The saddest are these: It might have been!

Prompt: Whittier meant that it's better to try something than to give up and wonder later if you might have succeeded. How might you apply this to your own life?

⊘ DECEMBER 18 ⊘

The 13th Amendment to the Constitution was ratified today in 1865. This is the amendment that abolished slavery in the nation.

Prompt: Abolishing slavery was the first of many, many steps over the years toward the achievement of equal rights for blacks in America. Can you name any other events that helped African-Americans win the rights they deserve? Do you think we will ever have a country free from racism? Explain.

Today people come from all over to Oxaca, Mexico, to celebrate the Feast of Our Lady of Solitude, to visit the shrine set aside in her honor, and to remember lonely people everywhere.

Prompt: Do you know anyone who is lonely? (It might be an elderly person who has no family, or a child with no friends, or someone who has lost a loved one.) What might you do to make this day less lonely for him or her?

DECEMBER 19

Author Eve Bunting (*The Ghost Children, Fly Away Home*) was born today in 1928 in Maghera, Northern Ireland. She confesses that she lost her urge to write after one of her college English teachers flunked her. Then, many years later, something made her start again. Now she's the author of over 100 books. Her advice to kids who want to write: "Read, read, read, and keep a journal...for you to put everything in, your emotions, what you're thinking." Eve also said, "A writer really needs persistence and faith in herself."

Prompt: Have you ever felt discouraged because someone else didn't appreciate your abilities and/or made an unkind remark? Explain what happened. Why do you think this person acted this way?

Today is Underdog Day, which focuses on all unsung heroes and underdogs. An example of an underdog is someone running for mayor who no one thinks can win. An unsung hero is someone who does a lot with no recognition.

Prompt: Do you know any underdogs or unsung heroes? If this person were standing in front of you now, what would you say to him or her to show that you've noticed all that he or she does?

DECEMBER 20

A Shoshone Indian woman named Sacagawea died on this day in 1812. Few other women have been honored with statues and memorials as often as Sacagawea. Why? With her two-month-old son, she traveled with explorers Lewis and Clark, who were traveling west across the country. Sacagawea translated between Native Americans and the two white men. It is said the expedition would never have made it without her.

Prompt: Can you think of any other strong women in history who rose above the crowd?

Today is Mudd Day, in honor of Dr. Mudd, who was born today near Bryantown, Maryland, in 1833. Dr. Mudd was sentenced to life imprisonment after giving medical help to John Wilkes Booth (who was disguised and on the run after shooting President Abraham Lincoln). Dr. Mudd suffered greatly in prison for four years before finally being pardoned by President Andrew Johnson.

Prompt: Do you think Dr. Mudd was treated fairly? Explain your answer. Why do you think he was treated so harshly? Do you think Dr. Mudd would receive the same treatment today?

DECEMBER 21

Tonight is the longest night of the year, the winter solstice. It's also the first official day of winter.

Prompt: What is your favorite season? Write a poem to honor it.

The first full-length, animated, talking picture was shown today in 1937 in Los Angeles, California. It was Walt Disney's *Snow White And The Seven Dwarfs*.

Prompt: What animated movies have you seen? Which is your favorite?

⊘ DECEMBER 22 ⊘

Today in 1956, baby "Colo" was born at the zoo in Columbus, Ohio. He was the first gorilla to be born in a zoo and weighed just over 3 pounds—lighter than many bookbags!

Prompt: Some people say zoos are important because they let people learn about animals and let scientists study animals. But others say animals should never be taken from the wild. Do you think zoos are ever a good idea? Explain.

On this day in 1864, General William T. Sherman sent a message to President Abraham Lincoln from Georgia: "I beg to present you as a Christmas gift the city of Savannah." General Sherman meant that he had burned the entire city of Savannah to the ground at the end of the Civil War between the northern and southern States. He allowed his soldiers to steal anything they wanted from southern homes.

Prompt: Abraham Lincoln was fair-minded and worked for peace. Do you think he truly appreciated General Sherman's gift? If you were Lincoln, how would you have responded?

⊘ DECEMBER 23 ⊘

George Washington retired from the army today in 1783.

Prompt: What *do* Presidents do when they retire? Imagine you've been the President (and an Army General) for many years, and suddenly you're retired. Make up a list of all the things you finally get to do that you couldn't do before. Use your imagination!

Scottish writer Samuel Smiles was born today in 1812 in London, England. Smiles wrote this now famous line: "A place for everything, and everything in its place."

Prompt: What kind of person are you—one who agrees with Samuel Smiles, or one who doesn't? Give an example of your behavior (in school or home) that shows this.

Are you ready to do something good for yourself? January is the time to do it. Many organizations encourage people to take on a special mission this month. Their ideas include:

- National Hot Tea Month
- National Book Blitz Month
- National Eye Care Month
- National Soup Month
- Oatmeal Month
- National Hobby Month
- National Cut (Back On) the Fat Month

Prompt: Pretend you've been hired for the month of January to run a campaign to promote one of the above ideas. Choose one of the ideas, then design your own campaign to teach people about it. A campaign can include ads in newspapers or on radio and television, slogans or mottos, songs, activities, etc.

⊘ JANUARY 1 ⊘

On this day in 1863, President Abraham Lincoln freed the slaves in most of the southern states. His freedom announcement was called the Emancipation Proclamation.

Prompt: Imagine you are a slave who has just heard President Lincoln's announcement. How would you feel? What would you do? If you could make one new rule to change life in the U.S. today, what would it be? Why?

Today is New Year's Day, when everyone has the chance to make a resolution, or promise, to give up or change a bad habit in order to improve his or her life. For example, people might promise to give up candy, read more often, or do homework first thing after school.

Prompt: Name two New Year's resolutions you'd like to make to improve your life and start the new year off right.

⊘ JANUARY 2 ⊘

In Haiti today it's Ancestors' Day, also known as Hero's Day.

Prompt: Do you have any ancestors you'd like to honor today? Some of our ancestors were heroes, some just seemed like heroes to the people who loved them. What qualities make a person a hero in your eyes?

Jean Little, author of *Lost and Found*, and *Mama's Going to Buy You a Mockingbird*, was born today. She started writing at the age of 10. She felt like an outsider as a kid, maybe because she had serious problems with her eyes (she is now legally blind). Because of her visual handicap, Jean often writes books about physically challenged children. But she confesses: "I write more for those children who are not [physically challenged], so that they can see that all children are really alike."

Prompt: Why do you think physically challenged children might feel like outsiders? Name three things other children might do to make a handicapped friend feel like part of the group.

⊘ JANUARY 3 ⊘

Alaska, which is sometimes called the Last Frontier, became the 49th state today in 1959. (The U.S. purchased the land from Russia in 1867.)

Prompt: Why do you think Alaska is called the Last Frontier? It might help to look up the meaning of "frontier" in a dictionary, and to look up a few facts about Alaska in the encyclopedia.

Today in 1847, the California town of Yerba Buena was renamed San Francisco.

Prompt: If you had a chance to rename your own town or city, what would you name it? Why?

⊘ JANUARY 4 ⊘

Isaac Newton is the physicist and mathematician who discovered the Law of Gravitation (gravity). The discovery started with an apple falling from a tree! Newton was born today in 1643 in Woolsthorpe, England.

Prompt: How do you think the apple taught Newton about gravity? Do you think Newton's discovery of gravity was important? Explain.

Today is Trivia Day, a day to celebrate people who know all sorts of facts.

Prompt: Do you know anyone who has a lot of facts in his or her head? Do you think those facts might ever come in handy?

⊘ JANUARY 5 ⊘

Today in 1931 in Rogers, Texas, dancer/choreographer Alvin Ailey was born. He founded the Alvin Ailey American Dance Theater, which created its ballets from classical ballet, jazz, Afro-Caribbean, and modern dance. Alvin's choreography helped to establish a role for African-Americans in the world of modern dance.

Prompt: Alvin Ailey was considered a pioneer. What do you think this means, considering he was a dancer and choreographer? Can *you* think of any other African-American pioneers? Describe their accomplishments.

Today begins Someday We'll Laugh About This Week! It reminds people to laugh at themselves once in a while.

Prompt: Did you know that it usually takes less than a week for people to break 9 out of 10 of their New Year's resolutions? Most people laugh at themselves when they do. Jot down a humorous story about yourself, and share a good laugh with a friend!

JANUARY 6

Poet Carl Sandburg was born today in 1878. He learned early that poetry couldn't support a wife and family, so he also worked as a journalist for the *Chicago Daily News*, as a traveling singer, a lecturer, and at the same time spent 16 years writing a six-volume biography of Abraham Lincoln.

Prompt: There are many kinds of writing, including poems, letters, newspaper articles, and fiction and nonfiction stories. What kind of writing do you like to do best? Why?

On this day hundreds of years ago, French people celebrated King of the Bean. A fancy cake was baked for the occasion and everyone at the party was given a slice. But only one of the slices contained a bean. Whoever got the bean became King of the Bean and everyone else had to do what he wanted for that day. Mary Queen of Scots later added a pea to the cake; whoever got that piece became Queen of the Bean and shared the throne with the King.

Prompt: Why do you think Mary decided to update this celebration by adding a Queen? What does this tell you about Mary's personal and/or political beliefs? Would you like to have an event like this at a birthday party?

JANUARY 7

Sherlock Holmes, the make-believe detective created by writer Sir Arthur Conan Doyle, was supposed to have been born today in 1854. Though he's over a century old, the character Sherlock Holmes has many fans who celebrate his birthday every year.

Prompt: Have you ever read a Sherlock Holmes mystery? Do you like mysteries and other scary stories? If so, who is your favorite scary writer? Why?

In parts of Japan, this day is called Rice Against Disaster Day or Nanakusa. On this day, rice is served with seven types of herbs as a charm against bad luck, disease, etc.

Prompt: Do you have a good luck charm (a lucky shirt, key chain, etc.)? How has it brought you luck?

JANUARY 8

Elvis Aaron Presley was born today in 1935 in Tupelo, Mississippi.

Prompt: Elvis Presley is sometimes called the King of Rock and Roll. Is there a musician you would call the King or Queen? (It doesn't have to be of rock and roll; it can be of any style of music you choose.)

Galilei Galileo died today in 1642 in Florence, Italy. He was the Italian astronomer who first put the telescope to use, and the first to discover that the moon had an irregular surface. He also discovered four of the satellites of Jupiter, the rings of Saturn, and sunspots. He was persecuted for believing (as Nicolaus Copernicus had declared years before) that the sun is the center of the solar system (not the Earth as was believed).

Prompt: Our century honors Galileo's genius and accomplishments, yet he was considered a foolish experimenter in his own time. Why do new ideas scare some people? Do you think people would have taken Galileo seriously if he had lived today?

◦ JANUARY 9 ◦

Today is Show and Tell Day at Work, when adults are encouraged to bring in a special object to the workplace and tell about it.

Prompt: What kinds of things do you think adults might present at show and tell? Pretend you are an adult you know who works. Imagine a show and tell object you think your adult would find interesting, and present it to the class as if you were that person.

Today in 1793, French aeronaut J. P. F. Blanchard carried an American flag as he took the first hot-air balloon ride in the U.S. George and Martha Washington were on hand to watch.

Prompt: Would you like to ride in a hot-air balloon? Would your answer change if balloons were a new invention and you'd be one of the first to go up?

◦ JANUARY 10 ◦

January 10, 1920, marks the anniversary of the League of Nations. The League was made of 50 nations that agreed to work together to avoid war. The United States never entered this agreement, and it was dissolved on April 18, 1946.

Prompt: Do you think the League of Nations was a good idea? Imagine how difficult it must have been for 50 nations to agree! Do you think this is why the League of Nations was dissolved? What do we have today that is like the League of Nations? (Hint: the word "Nations" is in its title too.) What else might countries do to avoid war?

On this date in 1878, Senator A. A. Sargent of California introduced the Women's Suffrage Amendment (also known as the Susan B. Anthony Amendment) into the U.S. Senate. When passed, this bill would give women the right to vote. The bill was finally signed into law 42 years later, on August 26, 1920.

Prompt: Why do you think it took so long for this amendment to become a law?

⚬ JANUARY 11 ⚬

Today begins a week of International Thank You Days, where people from all over the world are asked to thank someone they know today, or someone from the past who did something nice for them.

Prompt: If you could choose someone from the present or the past to thank, who would it be? What would you say to this person if he or she were standing in front of you now?

Today in 1964, the U.S. top doctor, Surgeon General Luther Terry, issued the first government report saying cigarette smoking may be hazardous to one's health.

Prompt: If you were in charge of a committee to find ways to discourage people from smoking cigarettes, what three suggestions would you give?

⚬ JANUARY 12 ⚬

British philosopher Edmund Burke was born on this day in 1729. One of his most famous quotes is: "The only thing necessary for the triumph of evil is for good men to do nothing."

Prompt: Tell what you think this quote means. Have you ever not spoken out about a wrong (for example, when someone was being mistreated) and later wished you had spoken? Explain what happened. If you could speak out now for a time you did nothing, what would you say?

Happy birthday, Charles Perrault! You may not know his name, but you probably know many of Perrault's stories. This Frenchman wrote the Mother Goose tales, including *Little Red Riding Hood*, *Tom Thumb*, *Sleeping Beauty*, and more. He was born on this day in 1628.

Prompt: Do you remember enjoying any Mother Goose stories when you were little? Which story was your favorite? Why?

⚬ JANUARY 13 ⚬

Today is National Clean-Off-Your-Desk Day, designed to be early in the year so that every desk worker can see the top of his or her desk and prepare for the following year's paperwork.

Prompt: Join in today's celebration and clean off your desk (at school and at home). If you can see the top of your desk already, then straighten up the inside! Describe what your classroom might look like if the desks were only cleaned once a year? Don't be afraid to use your imagination and have some fun.

On this day in 1808, Salmon Portland Chase was born in Cornish, New Hampshire. Chase was a Supreme Court Justice, or top judge. He was also one of the founders of the Republican Party and devoted much of his life to fighting slavery. His anti-slavery views kept him from being nominated for President in 1856 and 1860. You'll find Chase's face on U.S. $10,000 bills.

Prompt: Why do you think Salmon P. Chase's outspoken anti-slavery opinions caused him to be an unpopular candidate for President? If you could have your portrait on any piece of U.S. money, which one would you choose?

◦ JANUARY 14 ◦

In Bulgaria today it's Vine Grower's Day, an ancient holiday during which grape vines are pruned early in the morning and then sprinkled with wine from a decorated wooden holder. At this time everyone wishes for a great growing season. Later, there is a feast in a meadow complete with music, dancing, and horse racing.

Prompt: Think of something you'd like to celebrate. (It could be as simple as National Giggle Day or Summer Vacation Starting Day.) Next, make a list of ways to celebrate. (Include festivities, foods, special activities, type of dress or costume, etc.)

Today in 1734, in Yenesiesk, Siberia, the thermometers supposedly registered 120 degrees below zero. The air was so frigid, smoke couldn't rise in the air, and birds dropped frozen to the ground.

Prompt: What is the coldest day you can remember? Describe what it felt like as well as some of its effects on nature.

◦ JANUARY 15 ◦

Today is Dr. Martin Luther King Jr.'s birthday. King worked for racial equality and harmony in our nation.

Prompt: King's birthday is now a national holiday, and his peaceful efforts to ensure civil rights are remembered nationwide. Describe someone you know who shares Dr. King's beliefs, but is not famous. (It might be someone in your family, or a teacher or friend.) Tell what you admire most in this person.

Today is Elementary School Teacher Day, in honor of the men and women who work hard to bring knowledge to their children and to inspire them with encouragement and dreams.

Prompt: If you were an elementary school teacher, what three things would you most like your children to do to make your job easier today?

National Nothing Day is observed today to give Americans one day where they don't have to celebrate or honor anything!

Prompt: Considering all the holidays Americans celebrate, do you think this holiday is a good idea? Give the reasons for your answer. What is your favorite way of doing "nothing"?

Today in 1962, a mastodon (extinct woolly mammoth) skeleton was discovered by two 15-year-old boys in Hackensack, New Jersey. The boys found two huge teeth buried underground, and scientists later dug up the rest of this five-ton beast. It died at least 7,000 years ago.

Prompt: How do you think the boys felt when they found out the fossils belonged to an extinct creature? Write a short story explaining how the kids might have stumbled across the fossils. If you'd like, use this story starter: "It was the discovery of a lifetime. And it all started on a rainy Saturday afternoon..."

Ben Franklin, author, printer, scientist, diplomat, publisher, philosopher, and self-made, self-educated signer of the Declaration of Independence, was born on this day in 1706.

Prompt: What do you think the word self-made means? Do you know anyone with as many varied talents as Franklin? Describe what he or she can do.

Today in Mexico, people celebrate the Blessing of the Animals, where chickens, cows, and household pets are decorated with flowers and taken to the local church to be blessed.

Prompt: If you could organize a special day to honor pets (your own or a friend's), how would you and the pet(s) celebrate? What would you call this special day?

Peter Roget, English physicist and author of *Roget's Thesaurus*, was born today in London in 1779.

Prompt: What is a thesaurus? Find a thesaurus in a library, and look up a verb (such as eat or look). Explain how you think a thesaurus might be a valuable tool for writers. What other tools do writers need?

Chocolate Fest is celebrated today in East Towne Mall, Knoxville, Tennessee.

Prompt: Would you want to go to a chocolate fest? Why or why not? If not, what food would you put at the center of a big celebration?

⊘ JANUARY 19 ⊘

Today marks the first day of Celebrity Read a Book Week in Williamsport, Maryland.

Prompt: If you could choose any famous person (from the present or the past) to read a book to you, which book would you choose, and whom would you pick to read it to you? Why?

Edgar Allan Poe was born today in Boston, Massachusetts, in 1809. He was a critic, writer, magazine editor, and poet, and has been called, "America's most famous man of letters." Still, Edgar Allan Poe was not appreciated in America until after his death.

Prompt: Can you think of any other artists (painters, poets, singers, etc.) in America who were not truly appreciated until later in their lives, or even until after they had died? Why do you think this sometimes happens?

⊘ JANUARY 20 ⊘

Today in 1892 the first game of basketball was played in Springfield, Massachusetts. It was invented by James Naismith, who based basketball on a game called Duck on the Rock he'd played as a boy in Canada.

Prompt: What is your favorite sport to play? To watch?

In Breckenridge, Colorado, Ullr Fest is celebrated today to honor the mythical god of winter. Ice sculpture, parades, fireworks, and skiing, are all part of the festivities.

Prompt: Choose your favorite season, and name a festival after it. Explain how and where you would celebrate this festival. (Be sure to include activities that suit the weather and surroundings.)

⊘ JANUARY 21 ⊘

Today is National Hugging Day and should be spent hugging family members and friends.

Prompt: The Most Huggable People of the year are announced on this day. Make up a list of your own! Choose at least two people you think deserve this title (you may nominate yourself).

Confederate General Thomas Jonathan Jackson, one of the most famous soldiers of the Civil War, was born today in 1824.

Prompt: This General is better known as "Stonewall" Jackson. How do you think he got that name? If you're not sure, think about the two words that make up the name "Stonewall" and take a guess! Do you know anyone who has an interesting nickname? How did he or she get this name?

⊘ JANUARY 22 ⊘

Today is National School Nurse Day, which pays tribute to school nurses across the country.

Prompt: Think of three things you might do to make your school nurse feel honored and appreciated. You might interview her to find out all the duties she must perform in a day or a week especially those little extra things she does on her own. If your school does not have its own nurse, write a letter explaining why it could use one.

Did you know today is Answer Your Cat's Questions Day?

Prompt: Did you ever wonder what your cat, dog, or other pet was thinking about? Today, imagine a question your pet (or a friend's pet) might ask a human being. Then answer it in writing.

⊘ JANUARY 23 ⊘

On this day in 1849, Dr. Elizabeth Blackwell became the first woman to be awarded an MD (doctor's) degree. Although she was from Bristol, England, Dr. Blackwell received her degree from the Medical Institution of Geneva, New York.

Prompt: Can you think of another woman who was the first to accomplish something? If not, head to the library to research more women pioneers.

Today is National Pie Day, created to focus attention on pie as an American tradition.

Prompt: What is your favorite pie? Describe it in a way that would make everyone want to have a piece. How would *you* celebrate national pie day? (Name three ways.)

⊘ JANUARY 24 ⊘

Today is the anniversary of the California Gold Discovery of 1848, when James W. Wheeler (an employee of sawmill owner John Sutter) first saw gold in a tributary of the Sacramento River near Coloma, California. Although efforts were made to keep the discovery a secret, the famous Gold Rush soon followed. More than 200,000 gold seekers appeared at Sutter's Mill, hoping to find their fortunes.

Prompt: Think about all those people suddenly appearing in one spot! What would it take (if anything!) to cause you to drop everything and go to another part of the country?

It's three weeks into the new year, time to check up on your resolutions!

Prompt: Think of the resolutions you made at the beginning of the month. Have you stuck to all of them? Why or why not? Here's your chance to make new ones if the old ones were not practical.

⊘ JANUARY 25 ⊘

The first televised Presidential news conference happened today in 1961, when John F. Kennedy began a tradition of public meetings with the press. This tradition still survives today.

Prompt: Do you think televised news conferences with public officials is a good idea? Explain your answer. How do you think TV has changed the President's job?

Today begins National Scottish Culture Month. It's also the birthday of Scottish poet Robert Burns. This Scottish celebration includes bagpipe music and eating haggis—a traditional dish made of a sheep's or calf's liver, heart, lungs, onions and oatmeal.

Prompt: Can you think of any food that your family eats in celebration of your ethnic roots? If you can't think of one, describe a favorite dish that's made only for special occasions.

⊘ JANUARY 26 ⊘

Australia Day (or Foundation Day) is celebrated today to commemorate the founding of Australia by the British in 1788. Believe it or not, Australia was originally a place for the English to send their prisoners!

Prompt: After looking at a map, why do you think Australia is called the land Down Under? Write two questions you have about Australia, and research the answers.

Today in 1784, in a letter to his daughter, Benjamin Franklin complained about the eagle being the symbol of America. He wanted America's symbol to be the turkey!

Prompt: Would you have agreed with Ben Franklin? Why or why not? What do you think we'd be eating on Thanksgiving if the turkey had been chosen? What other animal might you suggest as a national symbol?

⊘ JANUARY 27 ⊘

The Vietnam War ended today in 1973 with the signing of an agreement in France between the opposing sides: The U.S. and South Vietnam had been fighting North Vietnam and the Viet Cong. It was the longest war in United States history and more than a million people lost their lives, including over 46,000 from America.

Prompt: Do you know anyone who fought in the Vietnam War? Do you think war has ever solved problems between two opposing points of view? What would you suggest countries do instead of war to resolve their differences?

Author Lewis Carroll was born today in 1832. He is most famous for writing *Alice's Adventures in Wonderland.* His real name was Charles Dodgson.

Prompt: Why might an author or movie star change his or her name? Would you change your name if you wanted to be famous? What would you change it to? Explain.

⟋ JANUARY 28 ⟋

Today in 1986, at exactly 11:39 a.m., the space shuttle *Challenger* exploded as it took off for space. All seven astronauts on board were killed. Among them was teacher Christa McAuliffe, the first ordinary citizen in space.

Prompt: Would you volunteer to explore space, knowing there is a tiny chance something like this could happen? Why or why not?

———————————

Author/illustrator of *A Chair For My Mother* and *More, More, More, Cried the Baby*, Vera B. Williams, was born today in 1927 in Hollywood, California. She believes that "drawing is one way of talking," and proves it by putting tape over her mouth when she visits schools. At first, she draws without speaking to show how an illustrator communicates through his or her pictures.

Prompt: Choose an emotion (or feeling), and try to express it only by drawing it. Don't worry about making mistakes. Just draw what you feel, using lines and colors to best express the emotion you've chosen. (Remember, it doesn't have to be a picture of anything if you don't want it to be.)

⟋ JANUARY 29 ⟋

Today is Oprah Winfrey's birthday. Oprah is a famous talk show host and owns her own multi-million-dollar company.

Prompt: Do you think Oprah is a good role model for kids your age? Why or why not? Would you like to be a talk show host, too? Why or why not?

———————————

Rosemary Wells, the author/illustrator of *Noisy Nora* and *Shy Charles*, was born today in 1943 in New York City. She believes that remembering what it was like being a child helps her to create stories that feel true—stories that stay interesting even after many readings.

Prompt: Choose a character name and an adjective; then create a title for a children's story such as "Hungry Hannah" or "Busy Bill." Then make up one incident that you think children might relate to (and maybe be helped by) if they read your story.

⟋ JANUARY 30 ⟋

Mahatma Gandhi, the Indian spiritual leader, was assassinated on this day in 1948. Gandhi believed in nonviolent resistance to achieve peace. He led his people (by his example) to freedom from British rule. He was mourned by the entire world.

Prompt: Can you think of any other great leaders who have died in the service of others, and whom the world still mourns today?

Author Tony Johnston (*Yonder* and *Whale Song*) was born today in 1942 in Los Angeles, California. She used to teach writing to fourth graders and believes there are always stories out there. You just have to find them. "You could walk around the block and find a story. It's the way you are in tune with the world around you that makes the difference," Johnston says.

Prompt: Do you think there's more than one way to find ideas for writing? Share one of the ways you get ideas.

✦ JANUARY 31 ✦

Jack Roosevelt (Jackie) Robinson, the first African-American to play major league baseball, was born today in 1919 in Cairo, Georgia. Jackie played with the Brooklyn Dodgers from 1947 to 1956. He was voted the National League's Most Valuable Player in 1949, and was elected to the Baseball Hall of Fame in 1962.

Prompt: It isn't easy being the first person to accomplish something in a public way. When Robinson began playing professional ball, other players and many fans spat at him and called him mean names. What qualities do you think Robinson must have had to overcome such obstacles?

Today in 1990, McDonald's opened its first fast-food restaurant in Russia.

Prompt: Sometimes McDonald's restaurants in other countries have different menus than the ones here in the U.S. For example, some McDonald's restaurants in Japan serve sushi, or raw fish. Do research to find out some foods eaten in Russia. Name at least one food you might serve at a McDonald's there.

FEBRUARY

Since 1976, February has been Black History Month, a time to recognize the many contributions African-Americans have made to United States history and culture.

Prompt: If you were asked to choose three African-Americans you think have contributed the most to U.S. history and culture, whom would you choose? Before making your choices, remember to consider the worlds of science, music, sports, literature, etc.

FEBRUARY 1

Today in 1865, President Lincoln approved the 13th Amendment to the Constitution (this amendment abolished slavery). In 1949, by Presidential Proclamation, this day became known as National Freedom Day.

Prompt: Can you imagine being a slave? Brainstorm for a few moments, then list three of the freedoms in your life that you hold most dear. Give your reasons for each choice.

Today begins National Snack Food Month in Alexandria, Virginia. It's a time to promote pretzels, potato chips, and other snacks.

Prompt: What are your favorite fun foods? (List at least three.) When do you most like eating these foods?

FEBRUARY 2

Today is Groundhog Day. The day is remembered especially in Punxsutawney, Pennsylvania. In 1887,

German settlers there began a tradition: They used this day to search for "Punxsutawney Phil, King of the Weather Prophets." Phil, of course, is a groundhog. If the sun isn't shining and he can't see his shadow when he comes out of his hole, there will be six more weeks of winter.

Prompt: People predict weather conditions or season changes in a variety of ways, some of them very funny. Can you think of some other ways to predict weather? Make a list.

Today in 1893, in Thomas Edison's newly completed Black Maria studio in West Orange, New Jersey, the first close-up in film history was shot—of a sneeze. It was appropriately called: The Record of a Sneeze.

Prompt: If you were going to film the first close-up in film history, what do you think your subject would be? Why do you think Edison chose a sneeze?

⊘ FEBRUARY 3 ⊘

In Japan, the custom of Setsubun has been observed for centuries to mark the last day of winter. It is based on a legend in which brave warriors throw soy beans into the eyes of demons to drive them away. Today, the demon is winter, and some Japanese spend the day playfully throwing soy beans at each other as a sign of driving winter away.

Prompt: Use your imagination to say good-bye to the season of your choice. Make up a custom for driving away that season and welcoming the next. Be sure to include any special actions or clothing.

Author Jean Lowery Nixon (*The House on Hackman's Hill* and *Land of Hope*) was born today in 1927 in Los Angeles, California. Jean says that some days when she's writing, words come into her head faster than she can write them down, yet on other days "it feels like every word comes out of [her] head with a pair of pliers."

Prompt: Which type of writing experience happens most for you: words coming too fast to write down, or pulling out each word with pliers? Explain how writing makes you feel.

⊘ FEBRUARY 4 ⊘

On this day in 1799 near Cambridge, England, 42-year-old Elizabeth Woodcock lost control of her horse and fell to the ground in the middle of a fierce snowstorm. By the time she heard church bells chime 8 p.m., she was buried under six feet of drifted snow. Elizabeth managed to push a thin branch through the snow above her with a handkerchief tied to its end, but no one discovered Elizabeth for eight days. She survived by eating snow.

Prompt: Do you have any interesting survival stories you can share? It could be an experience of someone you know or a story you have heard, or perhaps read about in a magazine or book. If you can't think of one, make one up!

Today in 1877, the Empress of Brazil presented a dress to Queen Elizabeth of England made from 700,000 spider webs. The dress was quite rare. Why? Although spiders produce beautiful silky threads, they are delicate and very difficult to work with.

Prompt: Brainstorm about different materials in nature that are not usually used to make fabric, then design an article of clothing from this material. For example, you might create a suit entirely of junk food, or a forest dress from acorns and autumn leaves. Explain who would wear it, and to what kind of event. Have some fun!

FEBRUARY 5

Today is Weather Person's Day, commemorating the birth of one of America's first weathermen, John Jeffries, in 1744. John Jeffries was a Boston physician who kept detailed records of weather conditions from 1774 to 1816.

Prompt: For Jeffries, keeping track of the weather started out as a hobby. Do you have any activities or hobbies that interest you? Can you think of a job or career related to your hobby?

Today in 1993, President Clinton signed the Family Leave Bill. This law requires all government agencies and companies with 50 or more employees to allow their employees to take time off to help with the birth or adoption of a child.

Prompt: Do you think this law is important? Why or why not?

FEBRUARY 6

Ronald Wilson Reagan, the 40th President of the U.S., was born today in 1911 in Tampico, Illinois. Actor, rancher, businessman, and author, Reagan was the first divorced person to become President—and also the oldest.

Prompt: What might be the advantages of having an older President? What might be the advantages of having a younger President?

On this day in 1895, George Herman Ruth (better known as Babe Ruth) was born in Baltimore,

Maryland. This left-handed pitcher hit 714 home runs and played in 10 World Series in 22 major league seasons!

Prompt: Do you (or does anyone you know) have a nickname? Where did this name (or names) come from? What's the most interesting nickname you have ever heard?

FEBRUARY 7

Today in 1954 in Shonto, Arizona, author/illustrator, Shonto Begay (*The Mud Pony* and *Ma'ii and Cousin Horned Toad*), was born. Shonto grew up on a Navajo reservation without running water or electricity. Instead of watching TV, he grew up hearing his grandmother tell stories. "A lot of [Navajo] teachings are explained through stories...stories are one way to preserve a good portion of your culture," Shonto says.

Prompt: Have you ever heard stories about people and events in your family's history? (It could be a story about how your parents met, or about how your great grandparents came to this country.)

The Great American Pizza Bake begins today! "Healthy" pizza is served in restaurants and pizza parlors nationwide to focus public attention on the importance of eating healthful foods.

Prompt: What is your favorite kind of pizza? Why? Do you think pizza can ever be good for you? Explain.

⊘ FEBRUARY 8 ⊘

Today begins National Forgiveness Week.

Prompt: Have you ever mistreated someone and would like to be forgiven? Tell why. Is there anyone you might forgive for harming you, even though it might be difficult for you? Explain.

The American Bowling Congress Championship Tournament begins today in Huntsville, Alabama, and hosts 50,000 bowlers from around the U.S. and several foreign countries.

Prompt: Did you know that bowling can be traced back to ancient Egypt and Polynesia (about 5200 b.c.)? In the 1100's in England it became more popular than archery! What do you think makes this game so popular?

⊘ FEBRUARY 9 ⊘

It is National Future Homemakers of America Week.

Prompt: How would you define a homemaker? Would you like to be one someday? Explain your answer.

The second week in February is also Random Acts of Kindness Week, to encourage people to do nice things for others.

Prompt: Name three kind acts you might do for a friend, family member, or neighbor. (For example, you might volunteer to do the dishes, walk a neighbor's dog, or even hold the classroom door open for someone.) What kind act might someone do to make you happy?

⊘ FEBRUARY 10 ⊘

Singing telegrams were introduced today in 1933 by the New York Postal Telegraph Company. A singing telegram is when a person delivers a birthday greeting or some other holiday message—in song.

Prompt: Choose an occasion (a relative's birthday, a friend's graduation, etc.) and design a singing telegram for that person and event. You may use an already written song or one you've made up yourself.

Author/illustrator E.L. (Elaine Lobl) Konigsburg was born today in 1930 in New York City. This author of *From the Mixed-up Files of Mrs. Basil E. Frankweiler* believes "the difference between being a person of talent and being an author is the ability to finish."

Prompt: Do you agree with Konigsburg? Have you ever started a project that you didn't finish? Did it bother you to *not* finish? Explain.

⊘ FEBRUARY 11 ⊘

Today in 1847, Thomas Alva Edison was born. Edison invented more than 1,200 items, including the light bulb and the phonograph (record player). He once said: "Genius is 1 percent inspiration and 99 percent perspiration."

Prompt: What do you think Edison's quote means? Do you agree?

Children's author Jane Yolen, creator of Owl Moon and many poems, was born today in 1939 in New York City. She says the greatest influence on her writing is the oral tradition of sharing stories by telling instead of writing them down. "I read everything out loud," says Yolen. "...I am hearing the story as music."

Prompt: Have you ever thought of the words in stories and poems as music? Choose a poem that you like. Read the poem silently to yourself, and then read it out loud. Do you feel a difference? Explain. Can you see why some authors read everything they write out loud?

❂ FEBRUARY 12 ❂

Abraham Lincoln, America's 16th President, was born today in 1809 in Hardin County, Kentucky. He was President when the Civil War was fought. Lincoln is credited with ending slavery in our country.

Prompt: Do you have a favorite U.S. President? Who is it? Give the reasons for your choice.

Judy Blume, author of *Superfudge* and *Tales of a Fourth Grade Nothing*, was born today in 1938 in Elizabeth, New Jersey. Blume says: "I think kids today rush from activity to activity.

When do they have the time to dream or play by themselves or just think? I don't know what happens when you don't have time to dream and think and play." Blume's books are usually about real things that happen to real kids.

Prompt: Do you agree that kids are rushed too much in today's world? Explain your answer. Describe something funny, sad, or embarrassing that has happened to you. Do you think other kids would like to hear your story?

❂ FEBRUARY 13 ❂

Did you know that today is Get a Different Name Day?

Prompt: Do you dislike your name or find it boring? If you could choose a different name for yourself, what would it be? Explain the reasons for your choice.

Today in 1635, the first public school in America, called the Boston Latin School, opened in Massachusetts.

Prompt: Can you imagine what it would be like to never go to school? Name three good things you have learned or received at school. (For example, learning to use computers or meeting new friends.)

❂ FEBRUARY 14 ❂

Everyone knows today is Valentine's Day. The practice of sending cards and love letters on this day comes from an old Roman feast.

Prompt: Do you give Valentine's Day

cards to friends and family? Do you like to receive cards? Why do you think people like Valentine's Day so much?

Today is Ferris Wheel Day, in honor of the American engineer who invented it, George Washington Gale Ferris. He was born today in Galesburg, Illinois, in 1859. He developed the first ferris wheel for the 1893 Columbian Exposition in Chicago, Illinois. This ferris wheel was huge (250 feet in diameter) with 36 coaches—each able to carry 40 passengers! It was a big attraction.

Prompt: Do you remember how you felt the first time you rode on a ferris wheel? Describe your experience. If you've never ridden on a ferris wheel, have you seen one? Was it daytime or nighttime? Describe how seeing a ferris wheel makes you feel.

⊘ FEBRUARY 15 ⊘

Susan B. Anthony was born today in 1820 in Adams, Massachusetts. Anthony fought for women's right to vote. In 1872, she was arrested and fined for voting. Back then, it was a crime! Anthony was also the first woman to have her image on a coin—the 1979 Susan B. Anthony dollar

Prompt: Can you think of any other rights and freedoms that women didn't have 100 years ago? Why do you think women were not allowed to vote back then?

Cyrus McCormick, the inventor of the reaper, was born today in 1809 at Rockbridge County, Virginia. The reaper made it easy for farmers to gather crops from their fields. Some say that McCormick's invention was almost as important as the railroad.

Prompt: How do you think farmers worked before the invention of the reaper? What three inventions do you think are most important? Why?

⊘ FEBRUARY 16 ⊘

Today begins National Engineers Week, when kids find out about engineers by visiting workplaces and having engineers speak at their schools.

Prompt: Do you know anyone who is an engineer? Do you know exactly what they do for a living? If you don't know what an engineer does, look it up at the library. Do you think you'd enjoy this job?

Today is Heart 2 Heart Day in Longwood, Florida. People are encouraged to start keeping a diary today.

Prompt: Some people say that over time their diaries become their best friends. Do you keep a diary or personal journal? If so, do you write in it every day? Can you see how when a person is lonely or upset, a diary can seem like a friend?

FEBRUARY 17

The third Monday in February is Presidents' Day, when the birthdays of George Washington (February 22) and Abraham Lincoln (February 12) are celebrated together.

Prompt: Why do you think the birthdays of Presidents Washington and Lincoln have been grouped together? Name one thing that's special about *each* man, to help remember both men as individuals. Do you think all Presidents should be honored on this day?

This week is International Friendship Week.

Prompt: What qualities do you look for in a friend? Name two things you might do this week to let a friend know how much you care about him or her?

FEBRUARY 18

Louis Tiffany, Jefferson Davis, Cybill Shepherd, Yoko Ono, Queen Mary I (Bloody Mary), Molly Ringwald, John Travolta, and Andrei Segovia were all born today on dates ranging from 1546 to 1968.

Prompt: How many names do you recognize from today's list of birthday people? Look up at least one of the names you don't recognize, and tell about that person.

Today Wisconsin celebrates Elm Farm Ollie Day, to commemorate the first cow to fly in an airplane. Ollie not only flew at the St. Louis International Air Exposition, she was milked and the milk (in paper containers) was parachuted over St. Louis! Although Ollie was from Missouri, Wisconsin residents celebrate the event by eating cheese and ice cream. Why? Wisconsin is the Dairy State.

Prompt: How do you suppose this unusual event came about? Make up a story!

FEBRUARY 19

On this day in 1848, Thomas Edison received a patent for his invention of the phonograph. For his work on the project, John Kreusi, Edison's assistant who made the machine from Edison's sketches, was paid a total of $18.

Prompt: If payment were made on such an invention today, how much do you think Thomas Edison would receive, and how much do you think John Kreusi would receive? Give your reasons for each amount.

Astronomer Nicolaus Copernicus was born today in Torun, Poland, in 1473. He changed science forever with his theory that the sun was the center of our solar system (back then, everyone believed the Earth was the center). He also introduced the idea that the Earth was moving (instead of standing still, as everyone had believed for 1,400 years). He was right!

Prompt: Why do you think people thought the earth was the center of the solar system for so long? If you're not sure, take a guess. Why do you think people believed the Earth was standing still?

FEBRUARY 20

Today in 1962, John Glenn became the first American (and the third man) to orbit the Earth. He rode aboard the space capsule *Friendship-7* and made three orbits of the Earth. Later, Glenn became a U.S. Senator.

Prompt: Which of Glenn's jobs would you prefer to have: astronaut or famous lawmaker? Why?

Today is Northern Hemisphere Hoodie-Hoo Day, when people are asked to go outside and yell "Hoodie-Hoo." Their shouts are supposed to chase away winter.

Prompt: Is there anything else you'd like to holler away (Homework? A rainy day?) Make up a word or phrase that works for you!

FEBRUARY 21

The 555-foot-tall Washington Monument was dedicated to our first President on this day in 1885 in Washington, D.C.

Prompt: Have you ever visited the Washington Monument? If so, describe your experience. If not, tell about your favorite monument. Is there anyone or anything you'd like to build a monument to? Explain.

Richard Nixon made his historic trip to the People's Republic of China on this day in 1972. He had meetings with China's leaders, Chairman Mao Tse-tung and Premier Chou En-lai. It proved to be the beginning of a new, friendly relationship between China and the U.S..

Prompt: It must have been difficult to meet with Chinese leaders after so many years of unfriendliness between the two countries. If you were Nixon, what would you have said to the Chinese leaders? What qualities would you need to have to make this meeting a success?

FEBRUARY 22

George Washington was born today in 1732 in Westmoreland County, Virginia. People have said Washington was "first in war, first in peace, and first in the hearts of his countrymen."

Prompt: Why do you think George Washington was considered to be "first" in so many areas of life? (Look up George Washington in an encyclopedia if you are not sure.) Then create a slogan that tells about you.

Today in 1956, 80 people were arrested during the Montgomery Bus Boycott. These people, including Rosa Parks and Martin Luther King, Jr., were protesting the mistreatment of black patrons on the city buses in Montgomery, Alabama.

Prompt: Would you be willing to be arrested for a cause you believe in? If so, what cause?

⦿ FEBRUARY 23 ⦿

Composer George Frederick Handel was born today in Germany in 1685. He is best known for his famous piece, *Messiah*, rumored to have been completed in only four days. A little-known fact about Handel is that his life was literally saved by music. During a duel, another musician named Mattheson stabbed Handel. But the sword broke after hitting the pages of music Handel had under his coat!

Prompt: Play a tape of Handel's *Messiah* (or another piece). How does the music make you feel? Describe it.

Today begins National Sign Up for Summer Camp Week.

Prompt: More than 6 million children attend day or sleepover summer camp each year. Have you ever been to summer camp? What was your favorite camp experience? If you've never been to camp, do you think you'd like to go? What would you most like to experience if you did go?

⦿ FEBRUARY 24 ⦿

Born today in 1786 in Hanau, Germany, was Wilhelm Grimm, one of the authors of *Grimm's Fairy Tales*. These tales are folk tales collected by Wilhelm and his brother from German farmers between 1807 and 1814. They include: "Hansel and Gretel," "Sleeping Beauty," "Little Red Riding Hood," "Snow White," "Cinderella," and "Puss-in-Boots."

Prompt: Which of the above tales do you like best? Explain why.

American artist Winslow Homer was born today in Boston, Massachusetts, in 1836. Homer illustrated Civil War battle scenes for a magazine. He also painted oils and water colors of farm and country life. He studied in Paris and the coastal town of Tynemouth, England, which centered his interest on the sea. His paintings of the sea brought him fame for their incredible sense of reality.

Prompt: Some of the things Homer painted were ones he had never seen. Have you ever done that? How would you go about painting something you'd never seen?

● FEBRUARY 25 ●

Italian singer Enrico Caruso was born today in 1873. He was so important to his country that people dedicated the world's largest candle to his memory in 1924. The candle is 18 feet high and 7 feet around, and is lit every year on Caruso's birthday. It is expected to last 1,800 years.

Prompt: Can you think of anyone you admire so much you'd burn a candle in his or her honor for 1,800 years? Explain what makes you like this person so much.

Cynthia Voigt, author of *Dicey's Song* and *The Wings of a Falcon*, was born today in 1942 in Boston Massachusetts. Cynthia admits she used to think that "smart people didn't make rough drafts or revise." Now she knows better, and revises many times before she's happy with a story.

Prompt: Like Voigt, some people think that smart people don't have to work as hard to succeed. Do you think this is true? Can you think of a time when you tried to skip steps or take the easy route? What happened as a result? What might have happened?

● FEBRUARY 26 ●

America's famous landmark, the Grand Canyon, was made a national park today in 1919.

Prompt: Have you ever seen the Grand Canyon or visited another national park? Describe your experience. Do you think people should have to pay money to see these sites? (This is a big controversy!)

Levi Strauss, the immigrant who created the first pair of blue jeans, was born today in 1829 in Bavaria, Germany. Levi's first jeans were made for California gold miners in the 1800s.

Prompt: Have you ever owned a pair of Levi's? Why do you think blue jeans were a good idea for gold miners?

● FEBRUARY 27 ●

Born in Philadelphia, Pennsylvania, today in 1897 was opera star Marian Anderson. In 1957, she became the first African-American to perform with the New York Metropolitan Opera. That success came after many years of suffering racial prejudice at the hands of fellow Americans. Anderson never gave up on herself. Eventually, she became a delegate to the United Nations, performed at President John F. Kennedy's inauguration, and, in 1963, received the Presidential Medal of Freedom.

Prompt: Marian Anderson is an example of someone who overcame racial injustice to achieve success in America. Can you think of any other African-Americans who did the same?

Beginning on the last Thursday in February, people on the Texas/Mexico border celebrate Charro Days. It's a celebration of the many ways Mexican culture has influenced America. Charro Days includes rodeo contests, piñatas, and much more.

Prompt: Can you think of anything in your everyday life that came to the U.S. from another culture? What might our country be like if we did not have such things? Explain.

FEBRUARY 28

Today marks the beginning of Bass Day, or Chalo Nitka (in the Seminole Indian language). Chalo Nitka promotes bass fishing in Lake Okeechobee.

Prompt: Do you know of any other Native American celebrations? Use books or an encyclopedia to help you find details of a celebration. Then share your findings with your class.

Asheville, North Carolina, celebrates its annual Comedy Classic weekend at this time of year. It reminds people of the importance of laughter to help get over everyday problems.

Prompt: What makes you laugh? A funny movie? Silly jokes? A favorite comedian or television show? Share what tickles your funny bone!

FEBRUARY 29

If this day is on the calendar, it is a Leap Year. Because of the way our calendar is set up, it occurs only every four years.

Prompt: Do you know anyone who was born on February 29? Would you like to have a birthday every four years instead of every year? Why or why not?

Leap Year was once was celebrated by an old tradition: On this day, unmarried women were expected to propose marriage to the bachelors of their choice. (Remember, in the old days, a woman never proposed marriage to a man.) In fact, in old Scotland, there was actually a law forbidding any man to turn down a woman who proposed to him on Leap Year! If he said no to a proposal, he was fined a large sum of money.

Prompt: What do you think of this old Leap Year tradition? Can you think of any other odd or interesting tradition that is no longer in existence today?

MARCH

March is National Women's History Month, a time for celebrating the contributions and achievements of women who have helped develop America, and whose accomplishments are too often overlooked in U.S. history books. Seneca Falls, New York (the town where the first Women's Rights Movement convention was held in 1848), is home of the National Women's Hall of Fame, which honors outstanding women contributors to sports, the arts, education, government, and science. Here are some of the women honored there:

- Abigail Adams
- Juliet Gordon Low
- Jane Addams
- Margaret Mead
- Marian Anderson
- Lucretia Mott
- Susan B. Anthony
- Alice Paul
- Clara Barton

- Eleanor Roosevelt
- Mary McCleod Bethune
- Florence Sabin
- Elizabeth Blackwell
- Margaret Sanger
- Pearl Buck
- Rachel Carson
- Elizabeth Cody Stanton
- Mary Cassatt

- Harriet Beecher Stowe
- Emily Dickinson
- Dorothea Dix
- Helen Brook Taussig
- Sojourner Truth
- Helen Hayes
- Harriet Tubman
- Helen Keller
- Babe Didrikson Zaharias

Prompt: How many of the above names can you identify? Do you know what contribution each woman made? Try making headings for arts, sports, education, etc., and see if you can place each name in the correct category. If you're not sure, you can look up the names you don't know in an encyclopedia. Or, choose one woman to research, and write an essay explaining how she contributed to history.

MARCH 1

Today begins National Nutrition Month, a great time to boost the amount of fruit and vegetables you eat and to cut back on sweets and fatty foods.

Prompt: Record your diet for one day. Then review everything that you ate. Did you get five servings of fruits and veggies? List the two "best" and the two "worst" foods that you ate. How might you improve your nutrition?

Irish-American Month begins today.

Prompt: Does your ethnic group have a day, week, or month when you celebrate your culture? Do you think every group needs its own time to celebrate? Explain.

MARCH 2

Theodor Geisel, better known as Dr. Seuss, was born today in 1904 in Springfield, Massachusetts. Dr. Seuss's first book, *And to Think That I Saw It On Mulberry Street*, was turned down by 27 publishers before it was published by Vanguard Press. Most famous for *The Cat in the Hat* and *The Grinch Who Stole Christmas*, Dr. Seuss won a Pulitzer Prize in 1984 for "his contribution over nearly half a century to the education and enjoyment of America's children and their parents."

Prompt: What do you think would have happened if Dr. Seuss gave up after the 26th publisher turned his first book down? What does this tell you about sticking behind something you believe in? What do you think young readers love about Dr. Suess's books?

Today begins Save Your Vision Week.

Prompt: Do you wear glasses? Has anyone ever made fun of you or a friend because of glasses? Why do you think people do this? Make up an appropriate, creative response to those teasers.

MARCH 3

Alexander Graham Bell was born on this day in 1847 in Edinburgh, Scotland. This inventor of the telephone got his interest in the transmission of sound from his father, Melville Bell, who was a teacher of the deaf.

Prompt: In addition to Bell, can you think of any other people whose accomplishments were influenced by a parent?

Today begins Newspapers in Education Week, to celebrate using newspapers in the classroom as "living textbooks."

Prompt: Have you ever used a newspaper in your classroom? What did you learn from it? Name at least one reason you think it's important for students to read the newspaper.

MARCH 4

On this day in 1984, the Television Academy Hall of Fame was formed in Burbank, California. Among the first people inducted into the Hall of Fame were Lucille Ball, Milton Berle, Norman Lear, Edward R. Murrow, and William S. Paley.

Prompt: Do you recognize the names of any of the first people inducted into the first Television Hall of Fame? If you were asked to nominate three individuals for this year's Hall of Fame awards, whom would you choose? Give your reasons for each choice.

March sometimes brings crazy weather. People have said that this month "comes in like a lion and goes out like a lamb."

Prompt: What do you think this quote about March means? Do you think it is true? Pick your birthday month, and write your own catchy phrase about its weather.

◎ **MARCH 5** ◎

Today is Stop Bad Service Day, when companies try to offer the best, most professional service possible. It's a good day to thank your favorite company.

Prompt: Make a list of all the services you use in a week. (Remember, restaurants, malls, movie theaters, and school lunch programs are all examples of service providers.) If you could thank one company for its great service to you, which one would you thank? Why?

Today is the first day of the Sandhill Crane (better known as the whooping crane) migration along the Platte River in Grand Island, Nebraska.

Prompt: Why do you think they are called whooping cranes? (Hint: Say the word "whooping" out loud.) Can you think of any other species of birds or animals who migrate (move from one part of the country to another during season changes)?

◎ **MARCH 6** ◎

Michelangelo, Renaissance painter, sculptor, architect, and poet, was born today in 1475 in Caprese, Italy. He is best known for his painting on the ceiling of the Sistine Chapel at the Vatican in Rome, and for his sculptures, *David* and *The Pieta*.

Prompt: Can you imagine yourself in a cramped, upside-down position painting a picture on a huge ceiling for nearly four years, and *still* creating one of the greatest works of art in history? Have you ever seen pictures of any of Michelangelo's works? What do you think of it?

On this day in 1938 in Chicago, Illinois, Thomas Garson ate 22 hamburgers and two quarts of ice cream in 25 minutes. Why? To win a bet. He did it for $40.

Prompt: Would you consider eating this amount of food on a bet? Would you bet someone else to do something this foolish? What's the silliest thing you've ever done on a bet (or dare)? What's the silliest thing you've ever asked someone to do?

◎ **MARCH 7** ◎

Today in 1876, Alexander Graham Bell was issued a patent for his "talking device."

Prompt: Name three ways life would be different if telephones had never been invented.

Liesch

EQUAL RIGHTS

Rattlesnake Roundup is celebrated today in Sweetwater, Texas.

Prompt: How would you celebrate a day that features rattlesnakes? (Name at least three ways). If you could celebrate the virtues of any animal in the world for a whole day, which one would you choose?

⊘ MARCH 8 ⊘

Celebrated today is International Working Women's Day. This holiday began in the U.S., but has been widely adopted by other nations, including Russia and China.

Prompt: Name a working woman whom you think deserves to be honored today. What kind of work does this woman do? Tell something special that made you choose her.

Today in 1911, the New York police introduced a new tool for catching and convicting criminals: fingerprints. Because of fingerprint evidence found at the scene of a crime, a man named Caesar Cella was convicted today of burglary.

Prompt: What do you think crime-solving was like before the use of fingerprint evidence? Can you think of any other devices (or methods) used today to help solve crimes?

⊘ MARCH 9 ⊘

In Belize (a small city in Central America), today is a public holiday: Baron Bliss Day. It seems this mysterious Englishman (Sir Henry Edward Ernest Victor Bliss) left his entire fortune to the city of Belize.

Prompt: What do you think caused Sir Bliss to leave his fortune to this city? Make up a story about it. If you were rich and could leave your entire fortune to one city or town, which one would it be?

Amerigo Vespucci was born today in 1451. America was named after Vespucci, even though he never achieved the fame of Columbus. Still, Vespucci's expeditions were very important because he knew he had discovered a new continent, not just a new route to the Orient (as everyone else was trying to do). Mapmaker Martin Waldseemuller is the one who named America for Vespucci.

Prompt: Whom would you rather be: Columbus, whom everyone thinks was the first explorer to land on American soil, or Vespucci, who probably was the first, and for whom our country is named? Why?

⊘ MARCH 10 ⊘

The first paper money was issued in the United States today in 1862, with Alexander Hamilton on $5 bills, Abraham Lincoln on $10 bills, and Liberty on $20 bills.

Prompt: Do you know who is on the $1 bill? (No peeking!) How about the $50? If you're not sure, look them up. If the U.S. were to create a new bill, whose face do you think should be on it?

The Most Boring Film Awards are celebrated today, with categories that include: Comedy, Action, and Big Stars-Big Flops.

Prompt: Please nominate three films you think should win the Most Boring Film award. Why did you find these films so dull? Do you think everyone in your class feels the same way you do?

⊘ MARCH 11 ⊘

Author/illustrator Ezra Jack Keats was born today in 1916 in Brooklyn, New York. Keats wrote *The Snowy Day* because he'd never seen a story about black children. According to *Horn Book Magazine*, it was the first full-color picture book to focus on a black child. Keats explained, "I wanted to show and share the beauty and goodness of the black child."

Prompt: Do you think it is important for readers to see characters in books who look like them? For example, if you were a girl and never saw a book about girls, how do you think you would feel?

Romeo Montevecchio was married to Juliet Cappelletto today in Cittadella, Italy, in 1302.

Prompt: Romeo and Juliet were real people, but they were also the subjects of a famous play by William Shakespeare. Can you think of any other books, plays, or movies that are based on real people?

⊘ MARCH 12 ⊘

Today is the anniversary of the Great Blizzard of '88 (1888, that is). The storm hit the northeastern U.S. with high winds and a snowfall of 40 to 50 inches. Some snow drifts were as high as 40 feet. More than 400 people died.

Prompt: What's the worst storm you ever heard about or experienced? (It does not have to be a snowstorm.) Share some of the details of this storm.

After being in office for only six days in 1933, President Franklin Delano Roosevelt broadcast the first of his Sunday evening Fireside Chats. During these chats, he spoke on the radio to the American people about the nation's problems and how he planned to deal with them.

Prompt: Do you think President Roosevelt's fireside chats were a good idea? Why or why not? Do you think they'd work as well today? (Remember, no one had a television back in 1933!)

⊘ MARCH 13 ⊘

Today is Good Samaritan Involvement Day, to stress the importance of helping others who need help.

Prompt: What do you think makes some people look away when a fellow human being needs help? What steps might you take to encourage people to help one another in your home or neighborhood?

Today begins Deaf History Month.

Prompt: Write down three questions you have about deaf history. Do research to find the answers to your questions.

● **MARCH 14** ●

Today is Moth-er Day; a day that honors moth collectors and specialists.

Prompt: Do you collect anything? What do you enjoy most about your collection? If you don't collect anything right now, imagine something you'd like to collect.

Save a Spider Day is today.

Prompt: How do you feel about spiders? Some people are scared silly. Do some research and find out one good fact about spiders.

● **MARCH 15** ●

New Jersey Songwriter's Show happens today in Waretown, New Jersey, where New Jersey's musicians come together to perform.

Prompt: If you were going to write a song, what would it be about? Which would you write first—the words or the music?

Trust Your Intuition Day is today. Intuition is when you say, "I just have a feeling that....," and you end up being right!

Prompt: Some people call intuition a gut feeling. Whatever it is, share one experience (of your own or of someone you know) where you think intuition was at work.

● **MARCH 16** ●

This day in 1621 marked the first visit of Native American Chief Samoset from the island of Monhegan to the new Colony of Plymouth.

Prompt: Try to imagine how such a meeting must have felt: 1) from the point of view of Chief Samoset, then 2) from the point of view of the Plymouth colonists. Remember, neither party had ever seen the likes of one another before; one was in a new land, and the other had always been there. Make a list of feelings and responses each side must have had, then compare them.

Today is Black Press Day in New York City, in honor of the founding of the first black newspaper in the United States, *Freedom's Journal*, in 1827.

Prompt: Share your impression of what it must have been like to speak the truth in a black newspaper in 1827. Do you think the title *Freedom's Journal* was a good name for this paper? Why or why not? If you were starting a newspaper that would focus on issues that are important to you right now, what would you name it?

MARCH 17

Today is St. Patrick's Day, in honor of the saint who died today in A.D. 464. The most famous legend about St. Patrick is that he drove all the snakes from Ireland by banging a drum. Today, St. Patrick's Day is a big holiday in many parts of the world. There are parades, and everyone wears green.

Prompt: Do you celebrate St. Patrick's Day? How? People say that on St. Patrick's Day, everyone is Irish. What do you think that means?

American singer Nat King Cole was born today in 1919. After he died, his daughter, Natalie, also became famous as a singer.

Prompt: Would you like to have a famous singer for a mom or dad? Do you think that having a parent who is a famous singer would make you feel extra pressure if you wanted to try your luck at singing? Explain.

MARCH 18

Today in 1944 in a Chicago department store, 2,500 shoppers trampled guards and floorwalkers in a panic to buy one of the 1,500 alarm clocks that were on sale. (Because of World War II, they had been unavailable until this day.)

Prompt: Can you imagine what it felt like to be in that crowd? Sometimes things like this happen today when there are only a certain number of special toys on sale, and many, many people at a store to buy them. What might be a fair way to sell the toys (or clocks) without making people mad?

John Luther Jones died today in 1900, in a crash of the Chicago and New Orleans Limited Railway. He stayed at the helm (or head) of the train, despite the certainty of dying, in order to slow down his speeding (and brakeless!) express train. He did this in an attempt to save as many lives as possible. He is now the hero of the folk ballad "Casey Jones." Here is an excerpt:

> Casey Jones, he mounted
> to the cabin,
> Casey Jones, with his orders
> in his hand!
> Casey Jones, he mounted
> to the cabin,
> Took his farewell trip
> into the promised land.

Prompt: Folk ballads record famous events (sometimes tragic, sometimes heroic) in rhyming song, so that people will always remember. Can you think of any other heroes (present or past), who have been remembered in a song?

MARCH 19

The U.S. Standard Time Act was passed today in 1918, setting up standard time zones for the United States. It also established Daylight Saving Time, which gives most of the U.S. an extra hour of sunlight each day during summer.

Prompt: Do you know which time zone you are in? Do you like the practice of Daylight Saving Time? If you could change it in any way, how would you change it?

Wyatt Earp was born today in 1848 in Monmouth, Illinois. He was a legend of the Old West, and had many occupations, including: railroad hand, saloonkeeper, gambler, lawman, gunslinger, miner, and real estate investor.

Prompt: Can you think of any other famous characters from the Old West? Look one up, and share some details from this person's life.

⊘ MARCH 21 ⊘

Today is the day of the Vernal Equinox. This is the beginning of spring in the Northern Hemisphere.

Prompt: If this is the beginning of spring in the Northern Hemisphere, what begins today in the *Southern* Hemisphere? Do you know what causes this difference in seasons? Name one thing you'd like to do today to celebrate the start of spring.

Author Lois Lowry was born today in 1937, in Honolulu, Hawaii. This author of *Number the Stars* once said that her purpose in writing for adolescents is "to make the reader feel less alone." She added: "Adolescence is often a painfully lonely time...a time when communication is difficult."

Prompt: Have you ever read a book that made you feel less lonely? What was it? What about this book helped you feel this way?

⊘ MARCH 20 ⊘

Noruz, or the Iranian New Year, starts today. Each household spreads out a special cover with symbols on it: sprouts, wheat germ, apples, hyacinth, fruit of the jujube, garlic, and sumac. Each symbol stands for something different: life, rebirth, health, happiness, prosperity, joy and beauty.

Prompt: How do you like to celebrate the New Year? Do you make resolutions? Eat certain foods? Sing special songs? Describe your favorite way(s) to celebrate this event. How do your celebrations compare with the Iranian celebration?

Today is National Teacher Appreciation Day for elementary through high school students to show appreciation for their teachers.

Prompt: Take a moment and think of three thoughtful ways you might show appreciation for a teacher. (Your three ways don't have to be money-bought gifts, they could be kind acts.)

⊘ MARCH 22 ⊘

In 1982, today became International Day of the Seal. The day was created to make people aware that if we continue to hunt seals, the creatures will probably become extinct.

Prompt: What would you say to someone who believes it's alright to hunt a creature that is near extinction?

Today is the birthday of Marcel Marceau, a world-famous mime. A mime is an actor who expresses himself only with movement. No words allowed!

Prompt: Have you ever seen a mime perform? (Many clowns are mimes.) Do you think it is a difficult job? Why or why not?

⊘ MARCH 23 ⊘

Today marks the first day of Norway's Easter Festival, which includes reindeer races. There is also a fair, concerts, and more.

Prompt: Many cultures are celebrating Easter (or a similar holiday) this week; each one with its own rites and festivities. Do you celebrate Easter? Which part of the celebration is your favorite? If you don't celebrate Easter, describe what you think is the best way to celebrate the coming of spring.

Patrick Henry, the American revolutionary leader, made his famous speech today in 1775 in the Virginia House of Delegates. His speech included the famous words: "I know not what course others may take; but as for me, give me liberty, or give me death!"

Prompt: What might Patrick Henry have been talking about? (Think about this period in U.S. history.) If you had lived in America at this time, do you think you would have agreed with him?

⊘ MARCH 24 ⊘

Today is Museum Day in honor of the 1937 Congressional approval of a National Gallery of Art in Washington, D.C. Congress declared that the gallery should belong to every citizen in the country, never charge admission, and be open every day of the year (except Christmas and New Year's).

Prompt: If you were appointed to start a museum, where would it be? What kinds of things would you put in it for people to come and see? What rules would you make for the museum and its visitors?

The first bombs ever used were thrown today in 1580 upon the town of Watchendonck, Germany.

Prompt: Do you think bombs were an important invention? How might our lives be different if they were never invented?

⊘ MARCH 25 ⊘

Pecan Day is celebrated today. Around this time in 1775, George Washington planted pecan trees (some are still alive!) at his home in Mount Vernon. The trees were a gift from Thomas Jefferson, but were first cultivated by Native Americans. The pecan is sometimes called "America's own nut," because it doesn't grow well anywhere else.

Prompt: What is your favorite nut? Why? Can you think of anything else that exists only (or mostly) in America?

EQUAL RIGHTS

A monumental day for music happened today in 1946, when Charlie "Bird" Parker played jazz (alto saxophone) at the Los Angeles Philharmonic Auditorium. His solo, "Lady Be Good," went down in history.

Prompt: Describe your favorite musical moment. (It might be the first time you heard your favorite song, when you performed your own solo, when you saw a musical, etc.)

MARCH 26

Poet Robert Frost was born today in 1874 in San Francisco, California. Frost tried his hand at farming, teaching, working in a textile mill, and newspaper editing—all the while writing poetry that didn't sell. But his determination paid off. He eventually won the Pulitzer Prize (one of the highest honors for a writer), and became the first poet ever to read at a Presidential Inauguration, when he read "The Gift Outright" for President Kennedy in 1961.

Another American poet, Walt Whitman, was also born today, in 1819. He too had many jobs, and, like Robert Frost, never gave up on writing poetry.

Prompt: Many American poets have not been recognized in their lifetimes. Can you think of something you love to do so much that you would never give up on it, even if no one paid you to do it?

MARCH 27

Patty Smith Hill, who wrote the words to the song "Happy Birthday," was born today in Kentucky in 1868. Some people think "Happy Birthday" has been sung more times than any other song in the world.

Prompt: What do you think made this song so popular? Do you think "Happy Birthday" is the most frequently sung song in the world? If not, which song would you choose?

Today is Photography Day, in honor of Edward Steichen, a photographer who lived in the mid-1900s.

Prompt: Do you like to look at photos in newspapers, magazines, albums, etc.? Do you ever take your own pictures? What would you photograph if you had a camera right now?

MARCH 28

Today in 1797, Nathaniel Briggs of New Hampshire received a patent for his invention, which he described as an "improvement for washing clothes." It was, of course, the washing machine.

Prompt: How do you think people reacted when they heard about Briggs's invention? What is your favorite invention?

Today in 1944 in New York City, singing commercials were banned by radio station WQXR.

Prompt: What is your favorite musical advertisement? (Think of all those jingles for soft drinks and fast food you often hum or carry around in your head.) If you were writing an ad, would you put it to music? Why or why not?

◎ MARCH 29 ◎

Today is Remembrance Day, to encourage us to remember a loved one who has died by planting a tree, performing community service, etc.

Prompt: What is community service? If you could perform an act of community service today in honor of someone who has died (it need not be someone you knew personally), whom would you choose to honor and what service would you perform?

◎ MARCH 30 ◎

Today in 1886, Coca-Cola went on sale for the first time in the U.S. It was advertised as a "brain tonic" and claimed to be able to relieve exhaustion.

Prompt: What is your favorite soft drink? Does it do what its ad says it will? Can you think of *any* product that matches the claims in its advertisements?

Dutch painter Vincent van Gogh was born today in Groot Zundert, Holland, in 1853. Spanish painter Francisco Goya was also born today in Aragon, Spain, in 1746. Van Gogh drew or painted more than 1,700 works of art, and Goya is credited with more than 1,800. Both men had influence on painters who were to follow, and both were artists whose ideas didn't always go along with the crowd.

Prompt: Do you know any artist (it could be a painter, poet, dancer, musician, etc.) who does not go along with the crowd? Tell who, and what you appreciate about him or her.

◎ MARCH 31 ◎

Today in the city of Luxembourg, *Emaishen* is celebrated. In the marketplace, sweethearts present each other with pottery that is sold only on this day.

Prompt: If you were in charge of creating a festival for sweethearts, where would you hold the festival? What gifts would sweethearts give to each other?

The Eiffel Tower was officially opened in Paris, France, today in 1889. Not everyone was happy about it: More than 100 leading composers, artists, and writers said the tower was ugly and didn't fit in with traditional French tastes or styles.

Prompt: What do you think is the ugliest monument or building you have ever seen? Where is it? Explain why you don't like it. Have you ever seen the Eiffel Tower (in person or in a photo)? What do you think of it?

APRIL

April is Keep America Beautiful Month, a good time to think about cutting down on trash, planting trees, and other ways to help the environment.

Prompt: Create a poster urging people in your community to "keep it clean." Be sure to provide some specific tips.

APRIL 1

Everyone knows today is April Fools' Day. But it has had different names in different countries: "Huntigowok Day" in Scotland, "April Noddy" in the north of England, and "Fooling the April Fish Day" in France.

Prompt: Describe the best April Fools' joke you've ever heard. Where do you suppose the April Fools' tradition of playing jokes came from?

Today in 1898, the first car (known then as a "motorized device") was sold in the United States. It cost $1,000 and was sold to Robert Allison by Alexander Winton, for whom it was named. The Winton could only go about 10 miles per hour (much slower than today's cars), and its engine was cooled by a block of ice.

Prompt: Name three ways our lives be different if no one had invented the motorized vehicle?

APRIL 2

Today is International Children's Book Day, which was designed to fall on the birthday of Hans Christian Andersen. Andersen was born today in 1805 in Oldense, Denmark. He wrote more than 150 fairy tales (including "The Ugly Duckling" and" "The Emperor's New Clothes"), which have delighted children around the world for over a hundred years.

Prompt: What is your favorite children's book? Write a book review. The review should include a summary of your book and a reason why others might enjoy it.

Frederic Auguste Bartholdi, the French sculptor who created the Statue of Liberty, was born today in 1834 in Alsace, France.

Prompt: Although Frederic Bartholdi died in 1904, do you think the world will ever forget him? Do you think Bartholdi created this statue so that he would be remembered? Explain your answer.

APRIL 3

The Pony Express began today in 1860. The first rider headed west from St. Joseph, Missouri. The second rider headed east from Sacramento, California. Each rider had a run of between 75 and 100 miles, with way stations (rest stops) every 10 or 15 miles.

Prompt: Look on a map and see if you can find where each rider started out from on that first day. Do you think the invention of the telegraph in 1861 changed things for the Pony Express? Look it up and find out what happened!

Today is the birthday of author Washington Irving (born in 1783). You probably know of Irving's famous story, *Rip Van Winkle*. Rip went to sleep for 20 years. When he woke up, he almost didn't recognize his own family!

Prompt: Imagine you were to fall asleep right now and stay asleep for 20 years. Describe what your experiences might be when you wake up and realize everything is different.

APRIL 4

Dorothea Dix, the American social reformer and author, was born today in 1802 in Hampden, Maine. Dorothea left home at age 10, was teaching at age 14, and founded a home for girls in Boston while still in her teens. She fought for better conditions in jails and homes for the poor and mentally ill.

Prompt: What makes Dorothea Dix a good role model for kids today? Is there a cause you would fight for? What makes you choose this cause?

Linus Yale, the inventor of the lock, was born today in Salisbury, New York, in 1821. He created the Yale Infallible Bank Lock as well as the cylinder lock.

Prompt: Imagine a time before people had to have locks. Now make up a story about the first person who ever needed a lock. (It can be funny or serious, or like a fable or fairy tale; it's your choice!)

APRIL 5

Booker T. Washington, the African-American educator, was born today in Franklin County, Virginia, in 1856. As soon as he was old enough, Washington worked in salt furnaces and coal mines. He also worked as a janitor at the Hampton Institute in exchange for three years of study. Washington was eventually chosen to organize a school for African-Americans which became Tuskegee Institute (in Alabama). In his autobiography, *Up From Slavery*, Washington wrote: "No race can prosper 'till it learns that there is as much dignity in tilling a field as in writing a poem."

Prompt: What do you think Booker T. Washington meant by this? Explain your answer.

Today is National Tomb Sweeping Day in Taiwan, where, according to Chinese custom, the tombs of ancestors are swept "clear and bright" as a sign of honor toward them.

Prompt: Do you think honoring one's ancestors is a good idea? Why or why not? Can you think of any other customs (from any country) where ancestors are honored? Describe one such custom.

● APRIL 6 ●

Children's author and illustrator Barbara Cooney was born today in 1917 in Brooklyn, New York. One of her stories, *Miss Rumphius*, is about a young girl who is determined to accomplish three things when she grows up: 1) visit faraway places, 2) live by the sea, and 3) do something to make the world more beautiful.

Prompt: Do you have any dreams for the future? Do you ever imagine yourself as a grownup working at a job, or as someone famous?

Today is Plan Your Epitaph Day, which corresponds with China's Ching Ming Festival honoring the dead. The point of this day is to honor yourself with an unforgettable epitaph, or gravestone saying.

Prompt: What would you like your epitaph to be? It might help to look up a few famous (and not so famous) epitaphs to get some ideas. Remember, an epitaph can be funny or serious.

● APRIL 7 ●

Today is World Health Day, which commemorates the establishment of the World Health Organization (WHO) in 1948. Its purpose is to help people all over the world lead healthier lives. WHO helps countries develop their own public health services and organizes campaigns against contagious diseases.

Prompt: If you were put in charge of Kid Health Day, name three (or more) things you would advise children to do in order to lead healthier lives.

April is Youth Sports Safety Month. This month, experts encourage children to wear helmets and other safety equipment when they play sports.

Prompt: Do you wear safety equipment when you ride a bike, skate, or play sports? Create a poster encouraging kids your age to use a bike helmet.

● APRIL 8 ●

On this day in 1513, explorer Ponce de Leon went searching for the fountain of youth. Instead, he landed on the coast of Florida (near what is now St. Augustine) and claimed it for Spain.

Prompt: If Ponce de Leon had discovered the fountain of youth, people's lives would be a lot different. Do you think this discovery would have been a great thing or a terrible thing? Explain your answer.

Today marks the day Hank Aaron of the Atlanta Braves hit the 715th homerun of his career and broke Babe Ruth's record set in 1935. Hank's record remains unbroken today.

Prompt: Do you know of any other great sports records? (They could be from any sport.) Which record would you most like to break?

APRIL 9

The Civil War ended today in 1865, when General Robert E. Lee, commander of the Army of Northern Virginia, surrendered to General Ulysses S. Grant, commander-in-chief of the Union Army, at the Appomattox Court House. The war lasted four years, and nearly 500,000 men died.

Prompt: The end of a war is a historic event. Do you think the problems that cause a war end when two opposing leaders sign an agreement? Do you think the problems that cause most fights in school or on the playground end when the fight is over? Explain your answer.

The Civil Rights Bill of 1866 was passed today by Congress (even though President Andrew Johnson had vetoed it). This bill gave African-Americans the rights and privileges of American citizenship.

Prompt: Can you believe that black soldiers fought for the Union Army in the Civil War (1861 to 1864), yet were not granted the right to vote or other rights of citizens? Imagine being asked to defend your country (and its freedoms) while not being allowed those same freedoms yourself. How would you feel?

APRIL 10

The Salvation Army celebrates its anniversary today on the birthday of its founder, William Booth. Booth was born in Nottingham, England, in 1829. He was a Methodist minister who began establishing mission stations (warm buildings with food and a clean place to sleep) to feed and house the poor.

Prompt: Name two things you can personally do to help those less fortunate than yourself.

Arbor Day was founded on this day in 1866 upon the suggestion by Governor Morton of Nebraska that the country declare a holiday to plant trees.

Prompt: If you were going to plant a tree, what kind would you choose? Where would you plant it? What else could you do to help the Earth's environment?

APRIL 11

Today marks the first day of the annual Ozark UFO Conference in Eureka Springs, Arkansas.

Prompt: List three questions you might have for a visitor from outer space.

Medieval Fair begins today in Norman, Oklahoma. This is a "living history" fair, where the Middle Ages are brought to life with jousting, music, and feasts of the time. It's a chance to meet such characters as King Arthur, Sir Lancelot, and Merlin.

Prompt: If you could choose your favorite time in history as the subject of a fair in your town, which time period would you choose? What events would you feature? What foods? What characters would you present?

● APRIL 12 ●

Today in 1853, the first truancy law was enacted in New York. Parents were charged a $50 fine if their kids (ages 5-15) were absent from school.

Prompt: Why do you think this law was first put into action? Do you think we could use such a law today? What do you think is the best way to tell the difference between a child who is truant (skipping school) and one who is home sick? Explain your answer.

The Salk vaccine was made available for the first time today in 1955. Developed by Dr. Jonas E. Salk, it was declared "safe, potent, and effective" against the crippling disease polio.

Prompt: Was this vaccine effective? Do you ever hear of anyone getting polio anymore? (It used to be like a plague; even the President of the United States, Franklin Delano Roosevelt, was not immune.) Can you think of any other vaccines that have saved lives?

● APRIL 13 ●

Today begins National Week of the Ocean, which focuses on the inter-

dependence between human beings and the ocean.

Prompt: What does interdependence mean? Name three (or more) ways we depend on the ocean. Explain how the ocean depends on us. What actions might you take to help this relationship?

Alfred M. Butts, the man who thought of the game *Scrabble* was born today in 1899, in Poughkeepsie, New York.

Prompt: What is your favorite board game? Why? Do you ever play a game that you or your friends made up? If so, explain how it is played.

● APRIL 14 ●

The *Titanic*, boldly declared the world's most unsinkable ship, sunk after hitting an iceberg today in 1912. Many mistakes were made leading to this disaster: 1) A lookout actually saw the iceberg, but the ship had ignored previous warnings and was moving too fast to avoid it; 2) Another ship ignored the *Titanic*'s distress signals; 3) There were not enough lifeboats to accommodate the number of people on the ship and many lives were lost.

Prompt: The *Titanic* voyage has captured the world's attention, from the day of the disaster to today. (Remember the 1998 hit movie?) Why do you think people are so interested in this disaster?

Anne Sullivan, Helen Keller's "miracle-working" teacher, was born today in 1866. Nearly blind herself, Miss Sullivan used a manual alphabet and communicated by the sense of touch to help Helen read, write, and speak—when no one else could reach her.

Prompt: Why was Anne Sullivan's teaching of Helen Keller so remarkable? Do you know any teachers whom you would consider remarkable? Explain.

APRIL 15

Today is Income Tax Day for all Americans; the deadline to pay our government the taxes we owe for the previous year. These taxes pay our share of the cost of government.

Prompt: Taxes pay for many things (fixing potholes, building highways, repairing bridges, keeping shelters open for the homeless, etc.). Pretend you were asked to decide two things for tax money to pay for in your community. What would you choose to fix or improve?

Today is known as Rubber Eraser Day, thanks to English chemist Joseph Priestley, who invented the eraser today in 1770. Priestley discovered that a small cube of latex (rubber) could rub out pencil marks.

Prompt: Can you think of any other small inventions that we take for granted? List five.

APRIL 16

Today is National Stress Awareness Day, to make the public aware that stress is one of the most serious health problems in the world today.

Prompt: Why do you think stress has become such a health problem? Do you think it was a problem a hundred years ago? Name two things (or situations) that stress you out the most.

Today is Thank You, School Librarian Day.

Prompt: Describe three services the school librarian performs for students, faculty, and parents in your school community. Brainstorm three ways you might show your appreciation.

APRIL 17

Author Martyn Godfrey (*I Spent My Summer Vacation Kidnapped Into Space*) was born today in 1949 in Birmingham, England. Martyn says he always writes the first two or three drafts of a book on his computer. Then he prints it and reads it out loud to a wall in his house. Then he takes it to a classroom of kids, leaves, and has the teacher read it for an honest response. Then he rewrites and rewrites.

Prompt: Every author creates in his or her own unique way. What happens when you write? Do you start on paper or computer? How many times do you usually rewrite a piece?

In Iceland today it's the First Day of Summer, or Sumardagurinn Fyrsti, a national public holiday that is celebrated with processions, street dancing, and flags.

Prompt: Where is Iceland? Find it on a map. Then look it up in an encyclopedia. Write three facts about Iceland.

● APRIL 18 ●

Today in 1934, the first launderette (then called a "washeteria") was opened in Fort Worth, Texas.

Prompt: How do you suppose people cleaned their clothes before washing machines and laundromats? How do you think we'll be washing our clothes in the year 2100? Use your imagination!

Spinach Festival starts today in Alma, Arizona.

Prompt: If you were hired by the state of Arizona to lead the spinach day celebration, how would you do it? (List some games, costumes, and spinach treats.) If you could choose a vegetable to organize a festival around, which veggie would you choose? Why?

● APRIL 19 ●

The Oklahoma City Bombing happened on this day in 1995. A federal office building exploded, killing most of the people inside (including some children at a day-care center). Kids all over the country have been writing letters to persuade the U.S. Postal Service to issue a commemorative stamp (America's Kids/American Hero Stamp) in honor of the 19 children who died in the bombing.

Prompt: Do you think this commemorative stamp would be a good idea? Explain why or why not. How else could people remember those who died in the blast?

Sheep to Shawl is celebrated today in Arrow Rock, Missouri. This festival shows the steps it takes to make a wool shawl: sheep shearing, wool carding, washing, dying, spinning, threading, and weaving. The entire process is completed by the afternoon!

Prompt: When we see sheep eating grass in a field, it rarely occurs to us how important they are to our warmth and comfort in chilly weather. Name two other animals that contribute in some way to making our lives more comfortable.

● APRIL 20 ●

Today is the first day of Intergenerational Week, which recognizes and promotes the special friendships between children and senior citizens.

Prompt: Have you ever had a friendship with an older adult? Explain the things that made your friendship different or special.

Today begins Professional Secretaries' Week.

Prompt: If you were a boss, what three things might you do to let your secretary know you value him or her? What might you do to make your school secretary feel more appreciated?

APRIL 21

Kindergarten Day is celebrated today, on the birthday of its inventor, Friedrich Froebel. He believed that play is an important part of a child's education.

Prompt: What is the most fun thing you can remember doing in kindergarten? Do you think you learned something from this activity? Explain.

Sky Awareness Week begins today, offering everyone the opportunity to stop and appreciate the sky's beauty, and to remind us to work together to protect this natural resource from air pollution and other threats.

Prompt: Draft a pretend letter to the president of a firm that pollutes the air. What arguments would you make to persuade the company to stop polluting?

APRIL 22

The first solo trip to the North Pole ended successfully today in 1994, when Norwegian explorer Borge Ousland reached the Pole. He pulled a 265-pound sled and averaged 18-and-a-half miles per day. It took Borge 52 days to make the 630-mile journey.

Prompt: If you could make a solo journey anywhere in the world, where would you choose to go? (Think carefully about your favorite habitats before you decide: deserts, rain forests, the ocean, mountains, etc.) Give the reasons for your choice.

Earth Day is here! This day was first celebrated in 1970, when kids and adults marched in parades and shared their concerns about our planet. Now we celebrate Earth Day every year on April 22.

Prompt: What do you think is the Earth's most serious problem? Why? What can kids and grown-ups do to help?

APRIL 23

William Shakespeare, one of the greatest writers of all time, was born in Stratford-on-Avon, England, today in 1564. He also died there today in 1616. Shakespeare led a quiet life, and wrote at least 36 plays and 154 sonnets (poems). It is a tradition on this day for people to place flowers on his grave.

Prompt: During his lifetime Shakespeare was known as "The Gentle Shakespeare," and is still remembered this way. How would you like to be remembered? Give yourself a name. (For example, "The Funniest William," or "The Most Courageous Anne.") Describe what you'd like to be remembered for.

Everyone has heard the old saying, "April showers bring May flowers." It's a great thing to think about this month.

Prompt: Is the old saying true so far this year? Has April been full of showers? If you could design a "perfect" day—weatherwise—what would it be? Who knows, maybe you'll get it!

○ APRIL 24 ○

Take Our Daughters to Work Day happens at this time each year. Many girls will go to work with an adult. This day has helped girls see a variety of possible careers.

Prompt: If you're a girl, have you ever felt left out just because you're a girl? Explain what happened. If you're a boy, have you ever noticed a situation where a girl has been left out just because she's a girl? Do you think it's okay to have a day when only girls go to work with their parents? Does that leave boys out? Explain.

Sham El-Nism is usually celebrated today (the date varies a little each year) in Egypt, and has been celebrated since the days of the pharaohs. This day translates into English as Sniff-The-Breeze-Day. People spend the day enjoying the fresh air as they picnic in parks or on the banks of the Nile River.

Prompt: If you could spend this day in any outdoor spot, which spot would you choose? Why?

○ APRIL 25 ○

The Hubble Space Telescope was deployed (sent into space) by the U.S. today in 1990. It can show objects up to 14 billion light-years away. The original Hubble lenses didn't work well and had to be fixed. In 1993, a shuttle crew went up, retrieved Hubble from orbit, fixed it, and returned it to orbit once more.

Prompt: Have you ever worked really hard on a project, only to discover it did not work? (Perhaps you forgot batteries, or a part was broken.) Explain what happened.

Today is National Good Telephone Day, a day when people are encouraged to answer the phone by the third ring, answer politely, and not leave anyone on hold.

Prompt: Can you think of any other ways to honor this day? (Before answering, think of what bothers you most when you're on the phone with someone.)

APRIL 26

Today marks a monumental day for South Africa: the anniversary of the first South African multiracial elections. In 1994, for the first time in the history of South Africa, the nation's approximately 18 million blacks voted. This marked the end of many years of white minority rule in that country. (Whites ruled the nation and did not let blacks even vote.)

Prompt: How would you feel if your class elected a class president, but only six students out of 26 were allowed to vote—and you weren't one of them? How would you feel if this happened during every election in your school for years?

Today in 1935 in Brooklyn, New York, writer Patricia Reilly Giff was born. This author of *The Polk Street School* used to be a teacher. She says she likes best the children who don't always get top grades or hit home runs.

Prompt: Can you think of a time when you failed at something, but kept trying until you could do it? How did you feel when you failed? How did you feel after you finally succeeded? Do you think you'd have felt this good if you didn't have to work at it?

APRIL 27

Samuel Morse, the American artist and inventor of the telegraph, was born today in 1791 in Charlestown, Massachusetts. The first telegraph line in the U.S. was between Washington, DC, and Baltimore, MD, where Morse tapped out the first message in 1844.

Prompt: If you had just invented the telegraph and were tapping out your first message, what message would you send? Explain why.

Ulysses Simpson Grant, the 18th President of the United States, was born today in 1822 in Point Pleasant, Ohio. His claims to fame were gaining the reputation of "Unconditional Surrender Grant" when he was in command of the Union Army during the Civil War, and still being in charge when General Robert E. Lee surrendered to him at the Appomattox Court House in Virginia.

Prompt: If you could give yourself a title to be remembered by—such as "Basketball-Loving Lena" or "Always-on-Time Avery"—what would your title be?

APRIL 28

The famous Mutiny on the Bounty happened today in 1789, in which the crew of the English naval vessel *HMS Bounty* mutinied, or turned against their cruel captain, William Bligh. The mutiny was lead by Fletcher Christian. Christian sent the captain and a few others out in a small boat and they were soon rescued. Christian and the rest of the crew ended up on an island. They remained undiscovered until 1808, when only one of the crew members was still alive.

Prompt: Fletcher Christian and his remaining crew lived in Tahiti for the rest of their lives. If you had been a member of the *HMS Bounty*, do you think you'd have chosen to go with Christian (and never return home again), or stay with cruel Captain Bligh (and possibly return home)?

The first parachute jump happened today in 1919 in Dayton, Ohio.

Prompt: Do you know anyone who performs daredevil activities (such as bungee jumping or parachuting) just for fun? Do you think you would enjoy such activities? Why or why not?

⊘ APRIL 29 ⊘

Today is the first day of Friendship Sees No Color Week, when everyone is encouraged to reach beyond color and make at least one new friend of another race.

Prompt: Give two reasons why you think celebrating this week is important.

On this date in 1913, Gideon Sandback of Hoboken, New Jersey, received a patent for his new invention, the zipper.

Prompt: Count in your mind all the items (not just clothing!) you use in a day that are fastened with zippers. Next, imagine what your life would be like if the zipper had never been invented. Make a list of the "little inventions" that mean the most to you.

⊘ APRIL 30 ⊘

Today in Sweden, the Feast of Valborg (also known as Walpurgis Night) is celebrated. This is when Sweden "sings in the spring" by singing traditional hymns, often around bonfires.

Prompt: Name one other celebration (from any culture) that uses fire or music. Why do you think people choose to celebrate this way?

Today is the start of School Spirit Season.

Prompt: Do you have school spirit? (Do you play on or cheer for your school's sports teams? Do you wear your school colors?) List five ways you and your friends could show more school spirit.

MAY

May is blooming with important events. Here's just a sampling of the things that are going on:

- Better Bike Month
- Breathe Easy Month (to promote lung health)
- Better Hearing Month
- National Arthritis Month
- National Barbecue Month
- National Sleep Month
- National Egg Month
- National Hamburger Month
- National Physical Fitness and Sports Month
- National Salad Month
- National Salsa Month
- Older Americans Month (formerly Senior Citizens Month)
- Project Safe Baby Month

Prompt: This is your May hit parade! Pick your favorite three causes from the above list. Then tell why these three are important to you. (For example, you might choose #4 because your grandma suffers from arthritis and you want her to feel better.)

MAY 1

May Day probably got its name from Maia, the mother of Mercury, who was honored in ancient Rome by celebrations of spring—with such activities as dancing around the Maypole or crowning a young girl Queen of the May.

Prompt: Is May Day celebrated in your town or neighborhood? If not, can you think of an interesting way to celebrate the coming of spring where you live? Make up an event that you think might welcome spring. Is there music? If so, what instruments are playing? What song? Be sure to include the details of any ceremonies or costumes or games.

Law Day is celebrated today to encourage people to support laws and respect law enforcement (the police).

Prompt: What does the statement, "No one is above the law" mean to you?

MAY 2

On this day the Kentucky Derby Day is often held. It is held on the first Saturday in May at Churchill Downs in Louisville, Kentucky. Here, thoroughbred horses race against each other while people bet money on the winner.

Prompt: Design a day of racing for any animal or self-propelling object: turtles, lawn movers, or in-line skates. Be sure to include rules—for qualifying, to decide winners, etc.—and have fun!

Today is International Tuba Day, to recognize tubists all over the world who have to go through the hassle of handling a tuba.

Prompt: Imagine going through a revolving door carrying a flute. Now imagine going through a revolving door carrying a tuba! Get the idea? Make a list of ordinary daily activities that become 10 times tougher to accomplish while carrying a big tuba.

MAY 3

Children's author Mavis Jukes was born today in 1947 in Nyack, New York. For five years Jukes was a teacher, then she studied to be a lawyer. Later, she discovered that as a writer, she had power to bring about change in society; especially by writing for young people.

Prompt: Do you agree with Mavis Jukes, that a writer can cause positive changes in people and society? Explain why you do or do not think so.

Bark in the Park Day is around this time at Lincoln Park in Chicago, Illinois. As part of Be Kind to Animals Week, thousands of people and their animals will be running or walking for this five-kilometer event.

Prompt: If you could sponsor a walkathon next Sunday for the worthy cause of your choice, what cause would you choose?

MAY 4

Today is National Weather Observer's Day, to honor people everywhere who love to watch the weather every day!

Prompt: Do you always pay attention to the weather before you go outside? What is your favorite type of weather? Why?

Today begins Conserve Your Water/ Detect a Leak Week.

Prompt: Leaks (even tiny ones) add up. One of the best ways to conserve water is by checking (and reporting) all leaks you find at home and at school. How else might you help in the fight to conserve water? List three or more ways.

MAY 5

The Republic of South Korea celebrates Urini Nal today; a special holiday for children. Schools are closed and parents plan special activities. On this day, the Children's Park in Seoul has free admission and offers great food and lots of activities.

Prompt: If you were in charge of planning Children's Day in the U.S., name five things you would do to make it a perfect day for kids.

Mexico's national holiday, Cinco de Mayo (The Fifth of May) happens today, honoring the 1862 battle in which Mexican troops were outnumbered three to one and still defeated the invading French troops of Napoleon III. This holiday is big: parades, festivals, and dances everywhere!

Prompt: Think of an important date in your life (besides your birthday). (It could be the birth of a little brother or sister, or the day you made the basketball team, or the day you moved to a new home.) Tell why you remember this day, then plan two activities to celebrate its anniversary every year.

MAY 6

Rabindranath Tagore, a Hindu poet, philosopher, and composer who won the Nobel Prize for Literature in 1913, was born today in 1861 in Calcutta, India. Tagore's songs and poems stirred pride among the people of his country.

Prompt: Can you name a poem (or song) that has made you feel proud of your country?

Babe Ruth's first Major League home run happened today in 1915, when he was playing for the Boston Red Sox against the New York Yankees.

Prompt: Think about an important first in your life. (Your first A in math, the first time you rode a two-wheeler, etc.) Do you still remember how it made you feel? Explain.

MAY 7

The Greek Philosopher Socrates died today in 399 B.C., after being sentenced to death for his controversial teachings.

Prompt: One of Socrates' most famous sayings was, "Know thyself." What do you think he meant by this? Name one thing *you* might do to know yourself better.

Beethoven's ninth symphony was played for the first time today in 1824 in Vienna, Austria. This is the one with the chorus singing *Ode to Joy*. Since Beethoven was completely deaf when he composed this symphony; he couldn't hear the cheers of the crowd after conducting. One of the soloists had to tug on his sleeve to get him to turn around!

Prompt: Do you ever hear music in your head when no music is playing? That's what it was like for Beethoven—he never let his deafness stop his music or his genius. Can you think of any other inspirational people who have overcome the obstacles of a physical handicap to live a normal (and sometimes extraordinary) life?

MAY 8

Today is the birthday of Harry S. Truman, the 33rd President of the U.S. Each year in Truman's honor, the current President participates in a Presidential Wreath Laying ceremony in which a wreath is placed on Truman's grave in Independence, Missouri.

Prompt: Think about the different Presidents you have studied or read about. If you could honor one of them by putting a wreath on his grave each year, which one would you choose? Give the reasons for your choice.

I n Denmark, today is the traditional day for storks to start arriving at Ribe to repair their rooftop nests and prepare for their new families.

Prompt: What is your favorite bird? Why is it your favorite? Tell about one of this bird's special habits. (Where does it live? When does it return in spring?) You might need to do some research before writing.

MAY 9

A uthor Eleanor Estes (*Ginger Pye*) was born today in 1906 in West Haven, Connecticut. She once said: "I like to make children laugh or cry, or to move them in some way." Eleanor felt a book was like a mirror for a child to look into and see a true image of what it is like to be a child.

Prompt: Can you think of a book you've read that was so true for you that it was like looking into a mirror? Did this book make you want to laugh or cry?

O n this day in 1754, Benjamin Franklin published the first American cartoon in his *Pennsylvania Gazette*.

Prompt: Do you have a favorite cartoon or cartoon character? Explain what you like most about this cartoon or character. Have you ever seen a political cartoon in a newspaper? Find one, and summarize the message in the cartoon.

MAY 10

N elson Mandela was inaugurated President of South Africa today in 1994. For 30 years, Mandela had been imprisoned because of his work for racial equality. Once he was released, he won South Africa's first free election easily.

Prompt: Pretend you are Nelson Mandela writing in your diary after this election. Explain how it feels to be victorious after spending so many years in prison for your beliefs.

T oday is National Windmill Day in the Netherlands. Although 950 windmills still survive, only 300 of them are still in use, and the government has named these national monuments.

Prompt: What do you think windmills are used for? Why do you think they've been named national monuments in the Netherlands?

⊘ MAY 11 ⊘

Mother's Day is celebrated on the second Sunday in May. It was first observed in 1907.

Prompt: Pretend you are someone's mother, and this is your day to have anything you want. What would you appreciate most from your child today? (Remember, some of the best gifts don't cost any money.)

Today is Eat What You Want Day.

Prompt: Here's your chance. Pretend you've been put in charge of designing a menu for Eat What You Want Day at your school. What foods would you serve? Don't forget to include some interesting beverages to accompany each dish!

⊘ MAY 12 ⊘

Today is Hummingbird Goose Day in Coos Bay, Oregon. Around this time, legend says, area geese allow tiny hummingbirds to burrow deep into their goose down. That way, the geese help the hummingbirds migrate north.

Prompt: Can you think of any other animals in nature who help each other? Describe how.

The odometer was invented today in 1847 by Mormon pioneer William Clayton while he was crossing the plains in a covered wagon. Prior to this invention, mileage was calculated by counting the revolutions of a rag tied to the spoke of a wagon wheel.

Prompt: Today, an odometer is used in a car. Describe how you might feel trying to count mileage the old way. Why do you think William Clayton invented the odometer?

⊘ MAY 13 ⊘

Today in 1954, President Eisenhower authorized construction of the St. Lawrence Seaway. It is the world's largest inland waterway, and permits ships to sail from the Atlantic Ocean to ports on the Great Lakes. It extends 182 miles from Montreal in Canada to the mouth of Lake Ontario. Both the U.S. and Canada took part in building the seaway.

Prompt: Look up the St. Lawrence Seaway on a map. Find the route ships would have to take if not for this short-cut. Do you think this seaway would have been built if the U.S. and Canada didn't cooperate to achieve this goal? Tell one way you've had to cooperate in order to achieve a goal this year.

Composer and musician Stevie Wonder was born today in 1950. Stevie has had one hit after another since he was 12 years old, despite his being blind. He also worked hard to make Martin Luther King, Jr.'s birthday a national holiday, and wishes there could be a party for world peace every year on this date.

Prompt: If you were famous, and

could use your influence to help a cause that you believe in, what cause would that be? Would you be willing to give your time for no pay (as Stevie Wonder has done) in order to achieve your goal?

MAY 14

Today in 1607, the first permanent English settlement in America got its start in Jamestown, Virginia. Led by Captain John Smith and Christopher Newport, 105 colonists arrived from Plymouth, England, on small ships: the Susan Comfort, the Godspeed, and Discovery.

Prompt: If you were traveling to a new world, and wanted to give your vessel just the right name (to bring you safe sailing and good luck), what would you call your ship? Give your reasons.

The first day of Midnight Sun begins today in North Cape, Norway. During this season, the sun never dips below the horizon.

Prompt: Do you think you'd like living in a place where the sun is always shining? In what ways do you think your life might change? (For example, would it make going to bed more difficult?) How would you feel living in a place that's always dark? Explain your answer.

MAY 15

Eastern Pacific hurricane season begins today and ends on November 30.

Prompt: Hurricanes are named for people. An alphabetical list of names is made beforehand, and each storm that comes along gets a name from the list. Choose two names (boy or girl) that you would give a hurricane.

Frank L. Baum, the author of *The Wizard of Oz* stories, was born today in 1856 in Chittenango, New York.

Prompt: If you could be any character in *The Wizard of Oz*, which one would you be? Explain why.

MAY 16

Today is Biographer's Day, celebrating the 1736 London meeting of James Boswell and Samuel Johnson. Boswell would go on to write Johnson's life story. It is one of the most famous biographies ever, and serves as a model to many writers.

Prompt: What's the difference between a biography and an autobiography? What's the most interesting biography you've ever read? If you could write a book about the life of someone you admire, whom would you write about?

The envelope, please.... Today in 1929, the first Academy Awards were given out. Now they are sometimes called Oscars. Each year, there is an award for Best Actor, Best Actress, Best Picture, and more.

Prompt: Think about your favorite films from this year, and make a list of your own Oscar winners for the categories listed above (plus any others you might come up with, such as Best Dog Actor!)

MAY 17

In 1954, this was a big day for civil rights in the courts: Thurgood Marshall argued against segregation in public schools and won in the case Brown vs. Board of Education. The Supreme Court ruled that segregation (separating white students from black students) denied an "equal educational opportunity" to black children. (Marshall later became the first African-American appointed to the Supreme Court.)

Prompt: Why do you think Thurgood Marshall's arguments in court were so important? How would you feel if you were told you couldn't attend a particular school because of the color of your skin?

Gary Paulsen was born today in 1939 in Minneapolis, Minnesota. This author of *Dogsong*, *Hatchet*, and *The Winter Room* tells kids very frankly about "the stupid things [he] did in the past." Gary feels that doing something wrong is not okay, and it's important to admit it. "I try to be as honest as I can," he says.

Prompt: When was the last time you made a mistake but didn't want to admit it? Explain what happened. Have you ever read any of Gary Paulsen's books? Which is your favorite? What did you like about it?

MAY 18

On this day in 1980, Mount St. Helens erupted, blowing steam and ash more than 11 miles into the sky. It was the first time this Washington state volcano had erupted since 1857.

Prompt: If you owned a home near a volcano that had been inactive for more than 100 years, but suddenly erupted, would you want to move? Or would you stick around and take your chances of facing another eruption? Explain.

This day is known as International Museum Day.

Prompt: What museums have you visited? Did you enjoy the experience? Do you think the Internet will make museums unnecessary, since kids can see artwork and many other things on their computer screens? Explain.

MAY 19

On this day in 1862, the Homestead Bill was passed, granting 160-acre lots of land to settlers who had resided on these lands for three years.

Prompt: If you could choose 160 acres of land to live on anywhere in the United States, where would you choose to live? (Be sure to consider if you want your land to be farm country, suburbs, city, beach, desert, etc.) You might wish to have a map of the U.S. in front of you while you decide. If you had three years to develop and work your land, what would you do with it?

L orraine Hansberry, the American playwright, was born today in 1930 in Chicago, Illinois. She was the youngest American (and the first African-American) to win the Best Play Award from the New York Critics' Circle for *A Raisin in the Sun*. This play dealt with the important issues of racism and cultural pride, and was the first stage production by a black woman to appear on Broadway.

Prompt: The title of Lorraine Hansberry's play comes from the opening lines of a poem by Langston Hughes called "Harlem":

> *What happens to a dream deferred?*
> *Does it dry up*
> *like a raisin in the sun?*

Since deferred means "put off until another time," can you see why Lorraine Hansberry chose this line as the title of her play? What dream do you think the poet—and, later, Hansberry—were referring to? Explain.

MAY 20

C harles Lindbergh became the first man to fly solo across the Atlantic Ocean today in 1929. Amelia Earhart became the first woman to fly solo across the Atlantic on the same date in 1932. Since Lindbergh was first to fly solo across the Atlantic, he got a $25,000 prize, became an instant world hero, and was given nicknames, including Lucky Lindy. Amelia Earhart, on

the other hand, missed out on the prize money and the nicknames.

Prompt: Do some research and write a news article about Amelia Earhart's accomplishment, as if it just happened. Be sure to give Amelia an appropriate "nickname."

T oday is National Bike to Work Day, on which biking to work is encouraged as a way to cut down on car fumes and help the environment.

Prompt: Do you think this is a good idea? What is your opinion of a National Bike to School Day?

MAY 21

C lara Barton founded the American Red Cross today in 1881. The Red Cross is an organization directed by volunteers. It provides disaster relief in the U.S. and abroad, and gives out donated blood to those in need.

Prompt: Everyone recognizes the red cross as the symbol of the American Red Cross organization. Do you know any other symbols? What do they stand for? Why might symbols be especially important for an organization that works in many countries?

Today is National Waitstaff Day, for restaurant managers and customers to show their appreciation of the many excellent waiters and waitresses who serve us all year long.

Prompt: If you were a waiter or waitress, what could you do to make your customers happy? What could customers do to make a waitstaff's job easier?

MAY 22

Arnold Lobel was born today in 1933 in Los Angeles, California. This author/illustrator of *Fables* and *Frog and Toad are Friends* once looked at one of his books and said: "I can't believe I did what I did." He was happy with his work.

Prompt: Have you ever looked at something you have done (a completed project, a great play in baseball, etc.), and felt the way Arnold Lobel did? Explain.

Today is the anniversary of the Battle of St. Albans in England in 1455. It is said that every year on this day, the houses on the site of the battle ring with the sound of clashing armor.

Prompt: Do you know any ghost stories? (They could be from history, or from family stories or encounters, etc.) If so, write one down. If not, make one up!

MAY 23

The New York Public Library was founded today in 1895.

Prompt: Do you go to a public library? What is your favorite thing about a library? List three things you could do at a library in addition to checking out books.

Author Scott O'Dell (*Island of the Blue Dolphins* and *Black Star, Bright Dawn*) was born today in 1898 in Los Angeles, California. The area where he grew up was a frontier town at the time. "It had more horses than automobiles, more jackrabbits than people," O'Dell said. The very first sound I remember was a wildcat scratching on the roof as I lay in bed."

Prompt: What's the very first sound that you can remember? What other memories do you have from when you were a young child?

MAY 24

Today in England, people are enjoying parades, fireworks, and big feasts. It is Commonwealth Day (also called Victoria Day), in honor of Queen Victoria, who was born on this day in 1819. Victoria ruled England for 64 years, and was greatly loved.

Prompt: How do you think a king or queen is different from an elected president? Do you ever wish our country had a monarchy (was ruled by a royal family)? Explain.

Today in Bulgaria it is a national holiday: Enlightenment and Culture Day, when everyone (schoolchildren, students, businesspeople, scientists, artists) shares their work with others to show their love for education and culture.

Prompt: What is culture? How might schoolchildren show love for education and culture? How might artists do the same thing? Name a way you might show your appreciation of your own culture.

⊘ MAY 25 ⊘

It's author Ann McGovern's birthday! Ann is a real-life adventurer who keeps a diary of each adventure, then writes a nonfiction book about it. Her adventures have taken her to every continent on Earth and led her to write more than 50 books for children. When she discovered scuba diving, it inspired her to write *Shark Lady* and *Night Dive*. Ann says she was afraid to scuba dive, but did it anyway, and fell in love with the underwater world.

Prompt: Have you ever been afraid to try something new, only to have it become a favorite thing to do? Explain how this happened and how it made you feel.

It's Freedom Day in Africa. In many spots on this vast continent, there are speeches, parades, sports, and songs today. There's also plenty of food, from nguba (peanuts) to baenge (sweet potato). Both words are from the Lokundo language, spoken in the Congo.

Prompt: Do you know any foods that have made their way from Africa to the United States? What about food from other places in the world?

⊘ MAY 26 ⊘

Dr. Sally Ride, the first American woman in space, was born today in 1951 in Encino, California. Her flight aboard the space shuttle *Challenger* lasted six days and was "nearly perfect." She is married to fellow astronaut Steve Hawley.

Prompt: Have you (or has anyone you know) ever been a first at anything? (A contest or a race? First string on a team? First born?) How does/did it feel?

Since 1943, the Tour of Somerville has been attracting top amateur cyclists to Somerville, New Jersey. This bicycle race happens annually on Memorial Day, the last Monday in May.

Prompt: A lot of kids own bicycles that mean a lot to them (no matter how old or rusty). In fact, a bike can seem like an old friend. Why do you think this happens? Have you ever owned a bicycle? If so, describe it. Then tell how you learned to ride it!

MAY 27

Julia Ward Howe, an American leader in the women's rights and anti-slavery movements, was born today in 1819. She is best known for writing the lyrics of the "Battle Hymn of the Republic."

Prompt: What is your favorite patriotic song? How does it make you feel? If you could go down in history as the composer of any song in the world, which song would it be? Why did you choose this particular song?

Rachel Carson, the author of *Silent Spring*, the book that made everyone more aware of ecology, was born today in 1907 in Springdale, Pennsylvania. Carson focused America's attention on its misuse of pesticides (chemicals used in farming) and their bad effects on living things. She caused important changes to be made.

Prompt: Can you think of a book that you've read that helped you see a situation differently? (It might be about ecology, history, or a family relationship, etc.) Describe how it made you change.

MAY 28

Today is National Senior Health and Fitness Day.

Prompt: What might you do to encourage an older American who is close to you to become fitter? Name two ways.

The Dionne quintuplets, the first quintuplets to survive more than a few hours, were born today in 1934 near Callander, Ontario, Canada. There were five girls: Marie, Cecile, Yvonne, Emilie, and Annette.

Prompt: Do you know anyone who is a twin or triplet? Do you think this relationship is different than one between brothers and sisters born separately? Explain your answer.

MAY 29

John Fitzgerald Kennedy, the 35th President of the U.S., was born today in Brookline, Massachusetts, in 1917. He was the youngest President ever elected. At his inauguration, Kennedy challenged the youth of America when he said: "Ask not what your country can do for you; ask what you can do for your country."

Prompt: If you were giving an inauguration speech tomorrow, and wanted to challenge the youth of America, what would you ask them to do?

American revolutionary leader Patrick Henry was born today in 1736 in Studley, Virginia. He is most remembered for these words: "I know not what course others may take, but as for me, give me liberty or give me death."

Prompt: If you were deciding whether or not to join the Virginia army to fight for your country's freedom from British rule, do you think Patrick Henry's words would inspire you to join? Now borrow Patrick Henry's phrasing and speak for yourself about something that matters to you. Fill in the blank:

   "Give me_____or give me death."

Don't be afraid to have fun!

MAY 30

The Hall of Fame for Great Americans, opened today in New York City in 1901.

Prompt: If you could nominate three people for this Hall of Fame, who would you nominate? If you could establish a Hall of Fame for Unknown but Still Great Americans that you know, whom would you nominate?

On this day in 1896 in New York City, the first automobile accident happened when Henry Wells's Duryea Motor Wagon collided with Evylyn Thomas, a bicycle rider.

Prompt: How do you think people reacted to that first car accident? Have you ever been in a car accident? Describe your experience.

MAY 31

National Save Your Hearing Day is today and focuses attention on the importance of safeguarding one's hearing.

Prompt: Our modern world presents constant challenges to our precious sense of hearing. One threat is the loud noise many people face every day. Name two loud things that might harm a person's ears, and two ways people can avoid hearing damage. (Hint: Think of technology like amplifiers and earphones.)

Today is National Time Out Day, set aside because no one in this day and age seems to have enough time to play with their children, read a book, or spend time with a friend. This is a day to do that one thing you never seem to have the time to do.

Prompt: Name that one thing you never seem to have the time to do. Name one thing an adult in your life never seems to have enough time to do. Why do you think this is so?

JUNE

June, traditionally the last month of the school year, is brimming with its share of themes including:

- Fireworks Safety Month
- Adopt a Shelter Cat Month
- June Dairy Month
- National Beef Steak Month
- Pest Control Month

- National Skin Safety Month
- Fresh Fruit and Vegetable Month
- National Frozen Yogurt Month
- National Iced Tea Month
- National Rose Month

Prompt: Can you tell what most of these themes have in common? Which one do you think is most important? Why?

JUNE 1

Today begins International Volunteers Week to honor people all over the world who offer themselves and their time to serve their communities—without payment.

Prompt: Have you ever volunteered to do a service for someone or donated your time to help others? Think of two ways you might offer your time at home and in the community to help others.

Roses Inside and Out is celebrated every Sunday in June in Granville, Ohio, at the Life-Style Museum, where family possessions featuring rose themes are displayed. Items on display range from embroidered tablecloths to hand-painted china and greeting cards.

Prompt: Pretend you've been asked to choose a living or non-living thing as the focus of a month-long celebration. What would you choose? Describe some of the items you plan to display.

JUNE 2

Something smells good! It's National Fragrance Week.

Prompt: Do you have a favorite scent? (It could be something as simple as vanilla or lilac.) Describe how it makes you feel when you smell it. If you were asked to create a new cologne just for kids, what would you make it smell like? What would you call it?

It's Washington's birthday again, but this time it's Martha's big day! Our first President's wife was born in 1832. She was a talented seamstress, cook, musician, gardener, and nurse.

Prompt: What do you think the job of First Lady is like (then and now)? Would you want it? How many First Ladies from history can you name?

JUNE 3

This day is celebrated in Virginia as Jack Jovette Day, in memory of the day in 1781 when Jack Jovette rode from the Cuckoo Tavern to Charlottesville, North Carolina, to warn Thomas Jefferson that the British were coming. Jefferson escaped to safety.

Prompt: Carrying an important message on horseback must have been tough. How would that same message get delivered today? Name at least three ways.

Today in 1888, one of America's most famous comic ballads was published in the *San Francisco Examiner*. Casey At the Bat. At first it appeared anonymously, but it was later claimed by Ernest L. Thayer. Here are two stanzas from the poem:

> *There was an ease in Casey's*
> *   manner as he stepped into his place;*
> *There was a pride in Casey's*
> *   bearing and a smile on Casey's face.*
> *And when, responding to the cheers,*
> *   he lightly doffed his hat,*
> *No stranger in the crowd could*
> *   doubt 'twas Casey at the bat.*
>
> *Ten thousand eyes were on him as he*
> *   rubbed his hands with dirt,*
> *Five thousand tongues applauded when*
> *   he wiped them on his shirt.*
> *Then while the writhing pitcher ground*
> *   the ball into his hip,*
> *Defiance gleamed in Casey's eye, a sneer*
> *   curled Casey's lip.*

Prompt: After reading the above stanzas from "Casey at the Bat," tell why you think this poem is still popular today.

JUNE 4

George III, the English king whose policies outraged the American

colonists until they rebelled, was born today in 1738. A result of these unfair policies, of course, was the American War for Independence, otherwise known as the Revolutionary War.

Prompt: If you were the King of England, and a colony was complaining about your policies, what do you think you would do? 1) Begin fighting? 2) Take a look at your policies to see if they are unfair.

Today in 1784 in Lyons, France, Marie Thible became the first woman in history to fly in a balloon. Marie was in such high spirits during her flight that she was heard "singing like a bird" as she drifted across Lyons. She reached 8,500 feet.

Prompt: Name an activity or event that would put you in such high spirits that you'd break into song. What song would you sing?

JUNE 5

Today we remember the World Campaign for the Biosphere. The biosphere is the Earth's crust and atmosphere—where all living organisms exist. The campaign is designed to awaken people to their responsibilities toward the environment.

Prompt: Some people threaten our planet by polluting it. Can you think of at least one way to help people stop spoiling our environment?

In Canada, the Shelburne County Lobster Festival begins today to celebrate the lobster fishing industry.

Prompt: Lobster fishing is a very important source of income for this section of Canada. What industry or occupation is important where you live? Explain.

JUNE 6

American patriot Nathan Hale was born today in 1755 in Coventry, Connecticut. During the Revolutionary War, Hale volunteered to spy behind enemy lines, and got caught. Just before he was hanged, he is supposed to have said these famous words: "I only regret that I have but one life to lose for my country." He was 21 years old.

Prompt: What do you think Hale's quote means? What is your definition of a patriot? Explain how someone your age might show patriotism in an everyday way.

Pet Appreciation Week is the second week in June.

Prompt: Think of three nice things you might do for your pet. (If you don't have a pet, this is your chance to imagine the pet of your dreams.) Then name three things your pet does for you.

JUNE 8

French painter Paul Gauguin was born today in Paris in 1848. Gauguin couldn't stand how poorly artists were treated, so he moved to the island of Tahiti. He is best remembered for his colorful paintings of Tahiti and its people.

Prompt: If you were going to leave tomorrow to spend your life in a distant land, which one would you choose? Give the reasons for your choice.

Today in Unionville, Missouri, people are celebrating the Festival of Trees, when old trees are honored on the courthouse lawn.

Prompt: Are there any very old trees in your area? How do they make you feel when you see them? If you do not know of any old trees, think of something else that's been around a very long time (a building, a mountain, etc.) and tell how seeing it makes you feel.

JUNE 7

National Flag Week begins today. All week, the American flag will be honored and the Pledge of Allegiance will be recited at public ceremonies. The week will end with National Flag Day on June 14.

Prompt: What are flags good for, anyway? Explain a flag's value to a country, state, or town. If you could design a flag to stand for you and your family, what would it look like?

Famous architect Frank Lloyd Wright was born today in 1867 in Richland

Center, Wisconsin. In his autobiography, Wright wrote: "No house should ever be on any hill or on anything. It should be of the hill, belonging to it, so hill and house could live together each the happier for the other."

Prompt: What does an architect do? What do you think Frank Lloyd Wright meant by the above quote? Describe (or draw) how you think Wright might have designed a house on a hillside.

JUNE 9

Today begins National Little League Baseball Week.

Prompt: Some people believe that parents and coaches put too much pressure on children who play Little League baseball. What is your opinion? Have you (or has anyone you know) ever experienced this kind of pressure?

Congratulations, Donald Duck! Our funny feathered friend was created by Disney on this day in 1934.

Prompt: Which Disney character do you like best: Donald, Mickey, Minnie, Pluto, Goofy, etc.? Which one is most like you? Explain.

JUNE 10

The singer and actress who played Dorothy in *The Wizard of Oz* was born today in Grand Rapids, Minnesota, in 1922. Her name was Frances Gumm before it was changed to Judy Garland.

Prompt: If you could click your heels three times (as Dorothy did in *The*

Wizard of Oz) and be transported to the happiest place you either remember or imagine, where would you go?

Today in 1652, silversmith John Hull established the first mint in America (against English colonial law) when he issued the first coin: the Pine Tree Shilling.

Prompt: Pretend you've been put in charge of designing a new coin. Think for a while, then describe: 1) what your coin would look like; 2) what it is made of (clay, a precious metal); and 3) how much the coin is worth.

JUNE 11

Author Robert Munsch (*The Paper Bag Princess*, *Giant*) was born today in 1945 in Pittsburgh, Pennsylvania. Robert didn't start out to be a writer; he worked in a day-care center, and told stories to the kids at naptime. He made up 519 stories in about two years. The children started asking for the same 10 stories over and over. When that happened, he knew these were the good ones. To this day, this is how Robert Munsch determines which stories to actually write down. He tells them to children first, and asks for their reactions.

Prompt: How do you determine whether something you've created is good or not? If you share it with someone for an opinion, with whom do you share? Have you ever thought something you've created is terrible only to find out later that other people like it? How did that make you feel?

Ben Jonson, an English playwright and poet born today in 1572, once said, "Talking and eloquence are not the same: to speak and to speak well, are two things."

Prompt: What do you think Ben Jonson meant by this? (If you need to, look up the word eloquence.) Even though it has been over 400 years since Jonson's statement, can you relate it to people and situations in your life today? Explain your answer.

JUNE 12

George Herbert Walker Bush, the 41st President of the U.S. (and 43rd Vice-President under Ronald Reagan), was born today in 1924 in Milton, Maine.

Prompt: President Bush outraged the broccoli industry and became popular with many children when he stated that he hated broccoli. Were you ever forced to eat a vegetable you didn't like? If you were President and could outlaw any vegetable you wanted, which one would you choose? Why?

The National Baseball Hall of Fame and Museum was dedicated today in 1939 at Cooperstown, New York.

Prompt: Do you have a favorite sports player you'd like to nominate for a Hall of Fame? (It does not have to be a baseball player.) Who is it? Explain why you'd like to nominate this person.

JUNE 13

The great Irish poet William Butler Yeats was born today in 1865 in Dublin, Ireland. His father, John Butler Yeats, was a well-known Irish painter, and it was thought for a while that William would be a painter too. But he discovered early that he loved poetry and drama. In 1923, he won the Nobel Prize for his writing.

Prompt: Many individuals try to follow in a parent's footsteps, only to find it's not right for them. Do you think Yeats would have won the Nobel Prize had he continued trying to be a painter? If you were a parent, would you want your child to be just like you? Explain your answer.

Today in 1927 in New York City, there was a ticker-tape parade for Charles Lindbergh in honor of his record-breaking solo flight in his plane: the *Spirit of Saint Louis*. During the parade, 750,000 pounds of paper confetti were showered all over Lindbergh and the city streets.

Prompt: In your opinion, who would appreciate a ticker-tape parade the least: an environmentalist or a paper manufacturer? Explain your answer.

JUNE 14

Author Laurence Yep (*Dragonwings* and *The Man Who Tricked a Ghost*) was born today in 1948, in San Francisco, California. Laurence read a lot of comic books as a child-then the *Wizard of Oz* books of Frank L. Baum. "In the Oz books, kids are carried away to a faraway place with strange customs. They have to adjust to survive." Laurence grew up in a black neighborhood, but went to school every day in Chinatown. "Every time I got on and off the bus, I had to adjust my reality. As a result, I feel like I could be dropped any place on Earth."

Prompt: Have you ever read a book that reminds you of your own life? What was it? How was it like your life? Do you think this book helped you in any way? Explain.

Today is Flag Day! It began in 1916 as a resolution by John Adams before the 1777 Continental Congress in Philadelphia, Pennsylvania. The rule said, "Resolved, that the flag of the thirteen United States shall be thirteen stripes, alternates red and white; that the union be thirteen stars, white on a blue field, representing a new constellation."

Prompt: Legend has it that George Washington asked a lady named Betsy Ross to sew the very first flag. No one knows for sure if this is true. Make up your own story about how the first flag came into being. (Be sure to include who made it, what it was made from, if it was made quickly or slowly or in secret, who saw it first, etc.)

JUNE 15

On this day in 1752, Benjamin Franklin performed his spectacular experiment of flying a kite during a thunderstorm to prove that electricity existed in lightning.

Prompt: Did you know that Benjamin Franklin invented a lot of things? Look up some of his inventions, and write down the three you feel are most important to your life today (you may include electricity).

In 1924, Congress passed an act making all Native Americans citizens of the U.S.

Prompt: What do you think of this act of Congress? If you were a Native American in 1924 (or now), how would the act make you feel? Explain your answer.

JUNE 16

On this day in 1963, Valentina Tereshkova became the first woman in space aboard the *Vostok 6*, launched from the USSR (now Russia).

Prompt: If you could be the first boy or girl to do something impressive, for what first would you like to be known?

Today begins Principals Week, designed for us to salute principals for all the work they do.

Prompt: If you were a principal, describe some of the work you would do (list at least five things). What might you do to show your principal you appreciate his or her efforts?

JUNE 17

The World Cup, the biggest tournament in soccer, is held at this time every year.

Prompt: Do you think soccer will one day be as popular here as football or baseball? Why or why not?

Every year around this time, the town of Smackover, Arkansas, has a festival to celebrate the town's biggest money-maker: oil.

Prompt: Does your town or state have a natural resource (like oil, coal, forests, etc.)? How do you think the discovery of oil or some other natural resource affects an area?

JUNE 18

Dr. Sally Ride became the first American woman in space today in 1983, when she traveled for six days aboard the space shuttle *Challenger*.

Prompt: How did Sally Ride's decision to go into space affect the lives of all American girls and women?

Go ahead and do what you want; it's Splurge Day! Splurging means buying or doing whatever you'd like.

Prompt: Pretend you won a shopping spree and had 10 minutes in any store to grab whatever you wanted, which store would you choose? What items are on your dream list? Who would you grab gifts for?

JUNE 19

Today we celebrate Father's Day. It was created by Presidential Proclamation in 1910. It was inspired by a YMCA worker, Mrs. John Dodd, with the rose becoming its official flower.

Prompt: Did you ever think to give a rose or other gift to your father (or to someone who is like a father to you) on Father's Day? Why or why not?

Garfield, the lasagna-loving comic cat created by Jim Davis, first appeared today in 1978.

Prompt: Who or what is your favorite comic strip character? Explain why you like him or her so much? If you could be any comic character in the world, which one would you be? Why?

⊘ JUNE 20 ⊘

Today is the anniversary of the Last Great Buffalo Hunt in 1862, when 2,000 Teton Sioux killed about 5,000 buffalo. This occasion is also known as The Last Stand of the American Buffalo, since within 16 months, the last of the buffalo were gone. Nearly 60 to 75 million of these creatures were killed prior to 1862 by white hunters.

Prompt: How do you feel about hunting? What rules (if any) should hunters have to follow?

Today is Day of Compassion, a day that television and radio stations dedicate to promoting compassion for individuals who are living with HIV and AIDS. This day was designed to educate and inform people about the disease.

Prompt: What could you do to help someone who is sick?

⊘ JUNE 21 ⊘

In the Northern Hemisphere, today is the first day of summer, or the summer solstice. But in the Southern Hemisphere, today is the beginning of winter.

Prompt: What's your favorite thing to do on a summer day? Why?

Today in Spivey's Corner, North Carolina, the National Hollerin' Contest is held. Hollering was an important means of communication in rural areas before the invention of the telephone!

Prompt: Name three occasions when

you think hollering (yelling loudly) would be useful for communication in the old days. What about today?

⊘ JUNE 22 ⊘

Anne Morrow Lindbergh, the American author and aviator, was born today in 1907. In her book *Gift From the Sea* she wrote: "By and large, mothers and housewives are the only workers who do not have a regular time off. They are the great vacationless class."

Prompt: Do you agree with this quote? Why or why not? Explain your answer.

For many students, this school year is just about over.

Prompt: List three important things you have learned this year. Then write a thank-you letter to someone who has helped you (teacher, parent, tutor, older sibling, study partner, etc.) throughout the year.

⊘ JUNE 23 ⊘

Movie madness is about to begin! Summer is one of the hottest times for new movies. Moviemakers know many children are out of school, so they release films that are aimed at kids.

Prompt: Think about the summer movies that are out right now. Which one(s) do you think are good for kids? Why? Which ones do you think aren't good? What is your favorite summer movie of all time?

In a speech made today in 1963, Martin Luther King, Jr. said, "I submit to you that if a man hasn't discovered something he will die for, he isn't fit to live."

Prompt: What do you think Dr. King meant by this statement? From what you know about Dr. King, do you think he felt this passionate about any issue? Explain.

JUNE 24

The first reported sighting of a flying saucer happened today in 1947 over Mt. Rainier, Washington.

Prompt: Do you believe in UFOs? Do you know anyone who claims to have seen one? Write a short story starting with these words? "I was out riding my bike over to my friend's house when I saw a green blinking light. At first I thought it was ..."

Celebration of the Senses happens today to remind people of the wonder of their senses: taste, touch, scent, sight, and sound.

Prompt: Which of your senses delights you the most? Why? If you had to give up one sense, which one would it be?

JUNE 25

Color television was introduced today in 1951. The first network to broadcast in color was CBS.

Prompt: Can you imagine life without color television? Can you imagine life without *any* television? What do you think you'd do instead? If you had to plan some no-television activities for your family, what would they be?

Custer's Last Stand happened today in 1876 at Little Big Horn River in Montana. Two-hundred-and-eight men died in this 20-minute battle lead by the Sioux chief, Sitting Bull.

Prompt: In the movies, Custer's Last Stand has always been presented as long battle in which the Native Americans are the bad guys and Custer is the good guy. Do some research, and decide for yourself if that's the way it happened. Write your own summary of the battle.

Biographical Index

Biographical Index